THE
TRINITY

The Triune
Nature of God

THE
TRINITY

The Triune
Nature of God

MIKE OPPENHEIMER

Lighthouse Trails Publishing
Eureka, Montana

Printed in the United States of America

Dedicated to all who have upheld the doctrine of the Triune God from the errors that began in the early church. And to those who continue to explain the Scripture on the eternal God who is unlike any other.

Also by Mike Oppenheimer

BOOKLETS

Did Jesus Identify Himself as God?

Israel: Replacing What God Has Not?

Chrislam: The Blending Together of Islam and Christianity

Understanding Paul's Appeal at Mars Hill

LECTURE DVDS

State of the World/State of the Church

Joel Osteen—The Smile of Deception

The "Gods" of the Nations—the God of Israel

The Need of Discernment in the Last Days

True Confessions of a Word-Faith Teacher—Joyce Meyer

The Gospel—What It Is, and What It Is Not

First Nations Movement

The Last Days, Israel, and Islam: Conflict of the Ages

Rick Warren's Panacea: A Fig Leaf P.E.A.C.E. Plan

CONTENTS

NOTE FROM PUBLISHER

Many books have been written by theologians and scholars on the subject of the Trinity. Mike Oppenheimer does not try to compete with these other efforts to explain one of the most misunderstood and seemingly complex doctrines in the church. Nor is his book an exhaustive study on the subject of the Trinity. Rather, he has tried to lay out, in a logical fashion and order, over 300 Scriptures with explanations of the various aspects of the Trinity. Our hope is that readers will be able to see this doctrine of the Christian faith as valid, vital, and well worth understanding and defending for the sake of the furtherance of the Gospel.

While this book may not answer all your questions about the Trinity, we hope and pray it will give you ample Scriptures from God's Word not only to see for yourself the truth of God—the Father, the Son, and the Holy Spirit—but also to share with others who are seeking to understand who He is.

1

CHRISTOLOGY

———————◆———————

If we are to grasp who God is, we must understand the core doctrine of the nature of God. Acceptance of the biblical view is what separates one from other views such as the polytheism found in Hinduism or the strict monotheism of Islam. How does God define Himself, and how do we explain and clarify the God of the Scriptures?

Since its beginning, the church (with the Scriptures as its foundation) has held that God is one, yet three persons *in* one. A lack of understanding on this subject does not justify the belief that God is Father only. We must acknowledge what has been communicated to us through the Scriptures—not that we have to understand it completely in every respect, but as believers, we need to apprehend what God has revealed through His holy Word.

The Jehovah's Witnesses, Mormons, Iglesia ni Christo, Christadelphians, and Oneness Pentecostals (Jesus Only) all have their own views of the character of the Son, all of which differ vastly from what the Bible reveals. A biblical understanding of the nature and character of the Son is crucial to understanding the nature and character of God.

The Trinity doctrine is criticized by many who claim it was developed hundreds of years after the apostles died and was not accepted until the fourth century. But an honest examination of church history clearly reveals the records of early church writings. As assaults against the primacy of the Scriptures were launched, godly men rose to the challenges to defend and affirm what the Scriptures themselves say.

Christology became the key to having a clear understanding of the nature and character of the Son. Was He merely a created being, or was and is He the Son of God, preexistent with the Father before He became incarnate as the man called Jesus?

The main argument used against the biblical view of the Trinity is that one cannot find the word "Trinity" in the Bible. Nor can there be found in Scripture the phrases "three persons" or "God the Son." The fact is, the word "Bible" is not in the Bible either. We use this word to describe all sixty-six books that make up our Old and New Testaments. Even chapter and verse numbers are not found in the original writings but came many centuries later, yet we accept and use them. We use these terms to explain biblical terminology to make plain what is written.

The Trinity doctrine was drawn from the Scriptures out of necessity to answer a series of errors, the first which was called modalism (oneness), a heresy that sprung up in the middle of the second century.

The word Trinity comes from the Latin word *trinitas*, which means three-in-one or threefold, much like the Hebrew word *echad* (a plural unity). The Trinity is not describing three substances but three distinct identities (persons) existing simultaneously, all of whom share the one essence of God. This does not mean they are three Gods nor are the persons separate from the essence; rather they abide as one *in* it. God is triune as persons but in nature is One. Athanasius coined the phrase in his debates, "not dividing the substance nor confusing the persons." In nature, they cannot be separated; in person, they have always been distinct in their identity but in relationship with each other. A. H. Strong stated:

> In the nature of the one God there are three eternal distinctions . . . and these three are equal. . . . "The doctrine of the Trinity does not on one hand assert that three persons are united as one person, or three beings in one being, or three Gods in one God (tri-theism); nor on the other hand that God merely manifests himself in three different ways (modal trinity, or trinity of manifestations); but rather that there are three eternal distinctions in the substance of God."[1]

While angels are called spirits, God is an uncreated Spirit, the One who created the angel spirits and the cause of all things existing, seen and unseen. God is not divisible among the distinctions of persons but indivisible. Distinguishing the differences of being and person can be related thus: "being" is what makes something what it is; it is its essential nature; "person" is what makes someone an individual identity. From the beginning, God has revealed Himself as one being that is plural in persons.

With no disrespect intended, in mathematical terms, the nature of God would not be 1+1+1 = 3, which would be tritheism, but rather 1x1x1 = 1, which would indicate a unified one. None of the persons of the Godhead can exist without the others. They all make up the one God in unity. However, if any one of the three appears, it is a God appearance. The essence is not wholly exclusive to only one of these at a time. Nor is it transferred from the Father to the Son (as if the Father becomes the Son or the Son becomes the Holy Spirit). All three have simultaneously existed together throughout eternity as the one God according to the Bible. Each person has a position and a relationship to each other.

2

ELOHIM

———————◆———————

The word for God appears in the Hebrew Bible over 2,500 times, and it has both a singular and plural form. In the singular, the Hebrew word is *El,* and it is often used as a connective word in describing God's characteristics or attributes (e.g., El Elyon, El Shaddai). For the plural form, the Hebrew suffix *im* (masculine in gender) is attached, giving us the word *Elohim* that is used throughout the Old Testament as the term for God. It is also occasionally used (small case elohim) in reference to false gods (plural). The use of the suffix im is also used in examples like seraphim (plural for seraph) and cherubim (plural for cherub).

However, it is not common practice in the Hebrew or the Greek texts to find nouns given a plural suffix as we do in the English language (mostly by adding the suffix "s"). In most cases, the same word is used for the singular and plural (like our word for "sheep" or "fish") where number is determined by the context of the sentence. All of this to say that the Hebrew word Elohim is unique in that it denotes plurality in and of itself.

So, grammatically speaking, El is the singular form while the word Elohim is a plural noun, but its usage throughout the Old Testament reveals an ambiguity, yet one that is consistent; when referring to God, it becomes evident that Elohim is a composite unity because Scripture maintains that God is one as seen in this example:

> Know therefore this day, and consider it in thine heart, that the Lord he is God [Elohim] in heaven above, and upon the earth beneath: there is none else. (Deuteronomy 4:39)

But when referring to false gods, elohim always means more than one god as in this phrase "... all the gods [elohim] of Egypt" (Exodus 12:12) or this verse, "Thou shalt have no other gods [elohim] before me" (Exodus 20:3).

These and a vast number of other Scriptures in the Old Testament verify that while the word elohim is a plural noun, when referring to God (capital "G"), it always refers to one God with an inference of a plural nature. This becomes evident right from the beginning of Genesis where God is introduced as Elohim: "God [Elohim] created the heaven and the earth" (Genesis 1:1). We learn very quickly that God is also "Spirit": "The Spirit of God [Elohim] moved upon the face of the waters" (v. 2). Then, in Genesis 1:26, we discover that God (Elohim) refers to Himself as "us" and "our": "Let us make man in our image." This plural form is consistently carried out throughout the Old Testament, but beginning with Genesis 2:4, we find the word Elohim commonly accompanied with the Hebrew word YHWH, rendered as Yahweh or Jehovah or translated LORD, as we find in the King James Version. Hence, the term "LORD God" means that God, our Creator and Lord, is a plural within His being.

Often in Sunday School, the Trinity may be explained by analogy to an apple, an egg, or a human being. Each example is given credence to the fact it consists of more than one part, yet is one entity. And while these examples are of some help in understanding how one thing may consist of various parts, these examples dwindle quickly when truly trying to understand the nature of God. For example, an apple consists of a core, the flesh, and the skin, but no one would venture to point to an apple skin and call it an apple. Nor in the example of a human would we find a part of his body having verbal communication with another. But God is not like that. Each person of the Godhead can think and communicate with the others. So when in Genesis 1:26 God says, "Let us make man in our image," this verse discloses independent thought and cooperation as a plurality in one Creator. Some say God is speaking with the angels in Genesis 1:26. However, the Bible refutes this in Isaiah 40:12-15 when speaking of God creating the world; it asks, "With whom took he counsel" because God would not seek counsel from created beings who are unable to create. Furthermore, the speaker and the others addressed in the act of creating are of the same image that man will be made in: "So God created man in his own image, in the image of God created he him" (v. 27).

Now one might say that because man is made in the "image of God" and we are body, mind, and spirit, we must be a "trinity" also. But the fact is that a human cannot separate himself into three persons, each working independently from the other and communicating with each other as God does.

We find from the Scriptures all the attributes of God belong to Elohim; they are also shared among the three persons who are Elohim. Each is called God individually. Collectively, they are also called God. They are spoken of as one God because of their unity.

Now when we get to the New Testament, the Greek word for God is *theos*. As mentioned earlier in this chapter, the Greek New Testament nouns typically are the same word whether singular or plural. And theos is such a word where theos is singular (referring to God) or plural (referring to false gods) depending on the context of the sentence. Consider, for example, Paul's writing to the Corinthians:

> For though there be that are called gods [theos], whether in heaven or in earth, (as there be gods many, and lords many,) but to us there is but one God [theos], the Father, of whom are all things, and we in him; and one Lord Jesus Christ, by whom are all things, and we by him. (1 Corinthians 8:5-6)

At the festival of Dedication (Lights) at Solomon's porch, Jesus is confronted by His people to tell them if He is the Christ (John 10:24). He responds by telling them "My sheep hear My voice." "I give unto them eternal life," "My Father, which gave them to me," and "I and my Father are one" (vv. 27-30).

Then when the Jews took up stones again to stone Him, Jesus asks, "For which of those works do ye stone me?" The Jews accuse Jesus of blasphemy "because that thou, being a man, makest thyself God." With all these statements and especially "I and my father are one" (vv. 30-33), they understood it all to mean He was claiming to be God; that is why they accused Him of blasphemy, with stoning as the punishment.

He answered, "Is it not written in your law, I said, Ye are gods [theos]?" (v. 34). Jesus was here reciting Psalm 82:6. He then goes from speaking in the plural to Himself in the singular. John 10:36 says, "say ye of Him whom the Father hath sanctified, and sent into the world, 'Thou blasphemest;' because I said, I am the Son of God? But Jesus now points out that His deeds are consistent with who He claims to be (vv. 37-38). His claim to be the Son of God cannot be blasphemy since He was sent to Earth and given the authority to do the Father's work.

The word theos can be applied to human judges and rulers as Jesus used it here even though they are not by nature God but represent Him in an authoritative capacity. However, they were *never* called Yahweh Elohim or I Am (as Jesus referred to Himself in John 8:58 alluding to Exodus 3:14-15); that name belongs to the one and only God, our Creator.

In conclusion, there is only one Supreme Being, who created all things, and we are not God nor are we a part of God. He is entirely separate from all creation, yet He is also the three persons of Father, Son, and Holy Spirit. In this life, we will never fully understand the Trinity, but Paul assures us that in eternity, "then shall I know even as also I am known" (1 Corinthians 13:12). But the way we can know Him now is as revealed by the Bible, and He is YHWH Elohim!

First John 5:20 says, "And we know that the Son of God is come, and hath given us an understanding, that we may know him that is true, and we are in him that is true even in his Son Jesus Christ. This is the true God, and eternal life" (see Deuteronomy 4:35, 39).

THE UNBIBLICAL ONENESS THEOLOGY

Oneness theology teachers say that 1) there is only one God; 2) God is numerically singular in person; 3) and Jesus Christ *is* the name of that one God. With Deuteronomy 6:4 as their proclamation, they reject any concept of unity within the one God that would change the numerical one from its strict singular meaning. Oneness theologians try to explain the oneness of God at the expense of the threeness. By using this as their beginning premise, they can only come to the conclusion that the three who are called God (the Father, Son, and Spirit) can only be singular in *person.* Interpreting that God is one as a strict numerical statement of His person, they make God become something He is not described as in Scripture. With both the Father and the Son being in the Old and New Testament, Oneness theologians must come up with an explanation of the relationship of both the Father and the Son in some other fashion. While they uphold the affirmation that Jesus is fully God and fully man, they reinterpret this to mean that the Father Himself is the deity in the Son, while the Son, in and of Himself, is strictly human. To put it simply in their terms, the Son is not God but only the man in whom God the Father dwells.—M.O.

3

THE WORD
"PERSONS"

◆

What makes someone a person? To begin with, he must possess the qualities and characteristics that make an individual personality, with identity, consciousness, and a conscience. The qualifications for a person are that he has a mind, a will, and emotions. God made man's nature in the image of God; He put in man qualities that He Himself has. So we reflect our Creator in a moral likeness (in our conscience).

A person is identified as a self-conscious being, cognizant of his own existence and of the existence of others who also have a self-identity. A "will" indicates the ability to think, to reason, and to make choices upon which to act. These are the qualities we associate with persons.

Speaking in human terms, for one to be called a father, he must have a son or daughter. This requires two individual persons in that it describes a relationship. Many interpret the Bible term "begotten" from the human standpoint of offspring. They apply the same begotten of humankind to the "only begotten Son" (John 1:18). Biblically, this does not mean a literal Father or Son but is communicating a relationship of love and communion. Both are eternal as the Son and the Father, meaning they are in this state of being individuals forever. No matter what other title (i.e., King, Priest, etc.) or function is applied to them, it does not change who they are as individual persons.

God is not a person in the same sense that we are persons with a physical body. Using the word "person" is an accommodation to our human language to show individual identity. The term "person" was chosen to convey the concept that the Father, Son, and Spirit each have their own consciousness and identity. The three have always been and will always be together in union as the one "Being" called God. When we hear such statements as, "the Bible never says they are three persons," it is an appeal to ignorance. As I explained earlier, there are many words that are not found in Scripture that are used to describe doctrines.

When we use the word person, we are distinguishing between who is who in identity. We are sure that Abraham, Moses, John, and Peter were different persons. When we read of angels such as Michael or Gabriel, we know they are individuals, persons (not the same angel). Yet nowhere does the Bible specifically say they are persons.

There is one God in nature of being, and there are three personal subjects; these distinct identities are recognized as persons.

If God is a *personal* being (not a human in origin, of course) then the Father, who is called God, is a person, an individual. So is the Son, who is also called God, as is the Holy Spirit. Therefore, if all three persons are called God separately, then when found together, are they not three persons who would be the one God? They are one God, not three Gods. Isaiah 43:10 says, "before me there was no God formed, neither shall there be after me," signifying that God is *one,* a unity, and there is no other.

Now, the word "change" describes something not retaining its own being, which certainly does not describe the God of the Bible who said, "For I am the Lord, I change not" (Malachi 3:6). In Hebrews, the writer quotes Psalm 102:25-27 on the subject of change (the Father speaking of the Son):

> And, Thou, Lord, in the beginning hast laid the foundation of the earth; and the heavens are the works of thine hands . . . and they shall be changed: but thou art the same, and thy years shall not fail. (Hebrews 1: 10, 12)

Only something created is subject to change, but the Son has always been coexistent with the Father, attributed to forming the earth and heavens by the Father, and will remain unchanged throughout all eternity.

We conclude, then, that the Son is a person who is part of the Godhead—uncreated, unchangeable, and eternal. Likewise, the Father and the Holy Spirit bear the same qualities and are persons abiding as one God while each retains His own individuality.

THE CRUX OF THE CHRISTIAN FAITH

No prophet, other than Jesus, could have said with authority, "he that believeth on me shall never thirst" or "He that believeth on me hath everlasting life" (John 6:35 & 47). No one but Jesus could have said with that same authority, "follow me" (Luke 18:22). Nor could any other prophet state, with signs and wonders proving His authority, that there are eternal consequences for not believing He is just who He claimed to be. When Jesus said, "for if ye believe not that I am *he*,* ye shall die in your sins" (John 8:24), it was the definitive statement of His very being. In fact, this declaration of His is the crux of the entire Christian faith.—M.O.

*The word "he" does not appear in the original (Greek) text but was added later in italics for readability.

4

THE PERSONHOOD OF GOD

———◆———

When we say that Father, Son, and Holy Spirit are all personal, we recognize necessary elements that constitute personality in each one. Each has a separate will, intellect, and emotions, which makes them different identities. These distinctions do not take away from their unity as one God. For example, it is the Son who became man and died for all mankind; the Father and the Spirit did not. The Son came in human flesh—while the other two never came in the flesh.

What we are *not* saying is that the persons are separate (as in three gods), nor are they physical persons. In speaking to the Samaritan woman, Jesus spoke of the Father when He said, "the true worshippers shall worship the Father in spirit and in truth" (John 4:23). He goes on to say in verse 24, God is Spirit, where, from the context, it is clear He is still speaking of God's nature It is significant to note here that the Father has the qualities of a spirit rather than a physical being (i.e., He is invisible and eternal). This is why Jesus can be called the fullness of the Godhead bodily (Colossians 2:9), yet God the Father is in Heaven. God cannot be divided—He is one God in His nature, yet the Father is not the Son, nor is the Son the Father in identity.

Each person of the Godhead is equal in essence, with none being superior or inferior in the essence of His nature. Positionally, they are different, having an order in the Godhead derived from Scripture. This can be demonstrated in that the Father sent the Son (John 3:16), and the Son glorified the Father (John 17:1), then after the Son is glorified, the Son sends the Holy Spirit who glorifies and points to the Son (Luke 24:49; John 15:26).

In 1 John 4:16, God is described as love (which is part of His nature that is eternal). Love is something that is given, but the *sharing* of love requires a giver and a receiver. Love is reciprocal where there is a relationship, and there needs to be an exchange. If God were only one person, He would have need of something outside Himself as the object of His love, but as a trinity, God is both love and sufficiency in Himself. In speaking of the Father, Jesus said, "[F]or thou lovedst me before the foundation of the world"(John 17:24). Here we find the Son as the object of the Father's love before anything existed. This is not a love of the future but was active and real, just as much in eternity past as it was in the New Testament time and as it is today. Both Father *and* Son are preexistent and eternal. To change this is to lose the biblical view of God found in Scripture.

WHO IS LORD?

The Scripture states there is one Lord (Ephesians 4:5). Yet we find the term Lord (Yahweh) applied to three persons, making them the one True God. All have the name Yahweh applied throughout the Old Testament. The New Testament concurs perfectly with all this in that the Father is Lord of Heaven and Earth (Matthew 11:25), and Jesus Christ is Lord (Philippians 2:10-11; 2 Corinthians 4:5). Jesus is called the Lord from Heaven (1 Corinthians 15:47) and the "Lord of all" (Acts 10:36). When He returns, He is called the "Lord of lords and King of kings" (Revelation 17:14). Looking back at Deuteronomy 10:17, we find that Yahweh is the Lord of lords—"For the Lord your God is God of gods, and Lord of lords." Only if Christ is Yahweh (the one true God) and the Father is Yahweh can we have no contradiction in Scripture. You cannot have two Lord of lords! Only a Trinitarian view of God eliminates the possibility of a contradiction. But what is most amazing about all this is that both the Old and New Testaments consistently uphold the idea that God is one and yet God is three persons. Deuteronomy 6:4 affirms there is one Lord, and there is one God, yet Paul, writing about the Holy Spirit, calls him Lord also.

> Now the Lord is that Spirit: and where the Spirit
> of the Lord is, there is liberty. (2 Corinthians 3:17)

All the authors of the Old and New Testaments wrote under the inspiration of the Holy Spirit and in so doing, saw no contradiction in the singular lordship of each of the Trinity because, as a trinity, they made up only one Lord.

JESUS IS THE SON

Jesus is called the Son over two hundred times through-out the New Testament. The Father is referred to as distinct from the Son over two hundred times. Over fifty times, Jesus the Son and the Father are mentioned together in the same verse, and He is always put on equal status with the Father when the Bible speaks of His nature. The apostle John speaks to this very issue when he declares:

> Grace be with you, mercy, and peace, from God
> the Father, and from the Lord Jesus Christ, the
> Son of the Father. (2 John 1:3)

Also in John 16:3 we find Jesus' declaration of being distinct from yet one with the Father when He states:

> And these things will they do unto you, because
> they have not known the Father, nor me.

These verses point to a Trinitarian view of God, and though Jesus is addressed as a distinct person from the Father, He is also given equal status with the Father.

Consider also 1 Thessalonians 1:1 and 2 Thessalonians 1:1, where it says:

> [U]nto the church of the Thessalonians in God our
> Father and the Lord Jesus Christ. (2 Thessalonians 1:1)

Notice it says the church is in both God the Father and in Christ also—the reason being that the Father and the Son are united, equal in nature. If Jesus were only human, then one would have to interpret these verses as the church in Christ's humanity and in the Father's deity. But that would make no sense. In the same way, Jesus says, "For where two or three are gathered together in my name, there am I in the midst of them" (Matthew 18:20). There are untold numbers of such gatherings all over the world, and He is with them all, in Spirit.

In John 10:30, 38, Jesus explained Himself as equal with His Father (even though He was a Son) when He said, "I and my Father are one" (John 10:30). Some use Jesus' statement "my Father is greater than I" (John 14:28) as "proof" that He is less than God. However, "greater" is the Greek word *meizoôn*; it is not referring to greater in *nature* or *essence* (as in John 10:30) but *position*. Remember that Jesus came to Earth as a servant, so He was less in His position, but He was still God in the flesh as pointed out again in 1 John 4:2,3,10,15.

When Jesus said the Father lives inside Him, He (the Son) is also in the Father (John 14:10; 17:21). He was making a point of their unique relationship that no other man has. They share equality in nature and being. They, as two, are essentially one in nature (not just in purpose); but they are not the same in person. This is what is meant by God being one. When Jesus said, "I and my Father are one" (John 10:30), this not a numerical reference. Jesus was not saying He is the Father. They are not the same in person, but in nature they are a united one. We see how His statement was interpreted by the Jews from the Pharisees reply, "[B]ecause that thou, being a man, makest thyself God" (John 10:33). They understood what He meant.

ALL THREE INVOLVED

In John 10:17-18, the Lord Jesus says, "I lay down my life, that I might take it again. No man taketh it from me, but I lay it down of myself. I have power to lay it down, and I have power to take it again." We are told the Father sent the Son to be the Savior of the world and the propitiation for our sin. We also read it was "in the power of the eternal Spirit that he offered himself without spot unto God." Here again in redemption the entire Trinity is involved.[2]—Harry A. Ironside

5

THE WORD "ONE"

There are some who take the Scriptures referring to God as being one and interpret them to mean God is one in person only; they ignore the plural statements. In the Old Testament, God is described as One. "Hear, O Israel: The LORD our God is one LORD" (Deuteronomy 6:4). This word for "one" is not a numerical one but actually implies a united one. The Hebrew word for one used in this passage is *echad*, which comes from the root word *ached*. Echad means to unify or collect together (the intensive reflexive form signifying "to unite." Echad is a unified one. Moses could have used the word *yachid*, which carries the meaning of an absolute numerical one. Despite all the explanations and anti-Trinitarian rhetoric, we can see they fail in light of the way the word "one" is consistently used throughout the Scriptures.

THE BIBLE DEFINES HOW THE
WORD ONE IS USED

In Genesis 1:5, evening and morning are first called one day (an example of echad, which combines two parts to make one). In the same manner, God says in Genesis 2:24 that Adam and Eve became one flesh—one in marriage, not as a person but in unity. In the New Testament, there is a Greek equivalent to the Hebrew word for "one." In Matthew 19:5, Jesus quotes Genesis 2:24 about a husband and wife becoming one flesh and the Greek word for one in that passage is *hen.* It is a neuter nominative, referring to one in essence and nature.

The concept of a united one is seen in Genesis 11:6 where God said, "Behold, the people [of the world] is one." In Psalm 133:1, the brethren are to dwell as one (in unity). In 1 Kings 11:13, Israel with twelve tribes is called one kingdom. Judges 20:8 describes unity as "all the people arose as one man." In Judges 20:11, it actually defines for us the meaning of one (that was used in Judges 20:8) by stating, "So all the men of Israel were gathered against the city, knit together as one man" (also see Nehemiah 8:1). In Numbers 13:23, when the spies went over into the land of Canaan, they brought back one cluster of grapes (Hebrews: Eschol echad), representing many grapes united as one. In all these examples, the word "one" is not singular. When applied to God, it is clearly used as a compound unity.

In John 17:21-26, Jesus prays that, as believers, we will be one, even as (in the Greek the word is *kathos,* meaning "according as," "just as," "even as") He and the Father are one, meaning united as in one body (a spiritual unity).

As believers, we have been given a new nature, can now understand His will and direction, and are connected to all other believers in His body in a spiritual way. We become one (united) in Him as a single body that spans the centuries. In Christ's prayer, He says:

> . . . that they all may be one; as thou, Father, art in me, and I in thee, that they also may be one in us. (John 17:21)

Here Jesus used the plural form, showing that this is meant as a spiritual union.

Paul also used this type of example of our unity as the church by illustrating that the spiritual gifts of the members must work together just as the parts of a human body must work together to the benefit of the whole—hence, a unity with many parts:

> For as the body is one, and hath many members, and all the members of that one body, being many, are one body: so also is Christ. For by one Spirit are we all baptized into one body. (1 Corinthians 12: 12-13)

He then goes on to emphasize that each of us is like a part of a physical body (e.g., eyes, feet, hands, etc.) forming a unity:

> But now are they many members, yet but one body. . . . Now ye are the body of Christ, and members in particular. (vv. 20, 27)

We are united as one but are still individuals in that one body.

The Old Testament uses a beautiful illustration for God as a compound unity. This example is found in the Jewish Passover Seder. The three-pocketed Matza bread holder used during Passover is referred to as a Yachatz, meaning "the unity." The Matza bread is unleavened, striped, and pierced. In the Passover service, the middle Matza is taken out of its white three-tiered holder and broken at a certain point during the ceremony. The smaller piece is left in its original holder, the larger piece is wrapped in a separate cloth to be hidden; it is called the Afikomen, the bread of affliction (referring to Isaiah 53:4; 63:8-9). This middle loaf is the only bread broken (Luke 22:19).

From the Messianic Jewish perspective, the Matza ceremony illustrates the tri-unity of God—the Father, the Son (middle matzoh), and the Holy Spirit (the Comforter) illustrating that Christ would be the "living bread" broken for us (John 6:51). So the middle piece of unleavened bread represents the Son, the second person of the triune God. As Jesus said in John 6:41:

I am the bread which came down from heaven.

In this ancient tradition during His last Passover, this is the bread Jesus broke and shared among His disciples. Matthew 26:26 records the event:

Jesus took bread, and blessed it, and brake it, and gave it to the disciples, and said, Take, eat; this is my body.

This breaking of bread accompanies the cup of redemption that Jesus said was the new covenant.

This unleavened bread symbolizes His body that was broken and afflicted, wrapped in strips of linen, and put in a tomb hidden from our view. As the bread is brought out from hiding, it is unwrapped (symbolizing His resurrection) and then eaten. It is a symbol of the Bread of Life shared with all who believe.

6

SON OF MAN—THE "SON OF GOD"

———◆———

I t is the Son that the cults and schismatics see as problematic. Anti-Trinitarians agree upon God the Father being God alone. In order to resolve their dilemma of refusing to acknowledge the Son as divine in nature, some try to say the Father became the Son. Others refuse to acknowledge the Son is equal in any respect.

There are two terms used to describe Jesus in reference to His deity—one directly, the other indirectly. The "Son of man" refers to His true humanity; the "Son of God" refers to His deity. God incarnated in His humanity, and a body was prepared without the human means of conception in which the Son would dwell (Hebrews 10:5; Galatians 4:4; John 1:14). The Son of God became the Son of man. These are different descriptions of His two natures.

In Luke 22:67-70, the Pharisees had the following discussion with Jesus:

Art thou the Christ? tell us. And he said unto them, If I tell you, ye will not believe: and if I also ask you, ye will not answer me, nor let me go. Hereafter shall the Son of man sit on the right hand of the power of God. Then said they all, Art thou then the Son of God?

Here Jesus is declaring He is the fulfillment of Psalm 8:4-6 (see also Hebrews 2:6-9) and the Son of man of Daniel's revelation (Daniel 7:13). Jesus asked, "What and if ye shall see the Son of man ascend up where he was before?" (John 6:62). Deity in humanity will be exalted to his rightful place. No man is able to sit in this position in Heaven. Yet He said in Matthew 24:30:

[A]nd they shall see the Son of man coming in the clouds of heaven with power and great glory.

The glorified Son of Man is seen by Daniel in a vision coming to the Ancient of Days, with the clouds of Heaven (v.13); this correlates with Revelation 1:7 as Jesus comes back to Earth (the clouds usually refer to glory). The phrase *one like the Son of man* in Daniel 7:13 is Daniel seeing Jesus in His post-resurrection form.

The term "Son of God" refers to His true and proper deity, being the Son from all eternity. Both terms refer to the same person—Jesus, who is the Son. Throughout the New Testament when Jesus uses the term "the Son of man" for Himself, it is in reference to showing the authority He had on Earth as a man. As the God/man, He's able to forgive sins (Mark 2:10), to execute judgment, to resurrect, and to call Himself the Lord of the Sabbath (Matthew 12:8). Near the end of his gospel, the apostle John states:

> [B]ut these are written, that ye might believe that Jesus is the Christ, the Son of God; and that believing ye might have life through his name. (John 20:31)

For one to have life in the Son, one must believe that Jesus was and is more than just a mere man or a good teacher but God in the flesh—pre-existent with the Father and who became man to redeem us.

UNDERSTANDING AN INFINITE GOD

It is beyond human capacity to comprehend the full nature of God's being. But neither can we understand what it means for us or anything else to exist—nor can we comprehend what space is or what time is or matter is. For every door science opens, there are ten more unopened doors on the other side. The more we learn, the more rapidly the unknown expands before us like receding images in a hall of mirrors. The Jehovah's Witnesses and other Unitarians argue that because the Trinity can't be understood, it can't be. But the fact that it is beyond human comprehension is no reason for rejecting what the Bible so consistently presents to us. God is telling us about Himself so we can believe in and know Him. We dare not reject what He says or lower it to the level of our finite minds.[3]— Dave Hunt

Mike's note: We see what is communicated and understand the infinite to a certain degree. Because one lacks understanding on this subject does not justify its rejection.

7

THE SON AS CREATOR

---◆---

> . . . who was faithful to him that appointed him, as also Moses was faithful in all his house. For this man was counted worthy of more glory than Moses, inasmuch as he who hath builded the house hath more honour than the house. For every house is builded by some man; but he that built all things is God. (Hebrews 3:2-4)

Jesus Christ is counted to have more glory than Moses, for "he who hath builded the house hath more honour than the house" (v. 3) and "For every house is builded by some man; but he that built all things is God" (v. 4). Moses was faithful as a servant in all God's house (v. 5). And in verse 6, it says, "but Christ as a son over his own house; whose house are we." Then in 1 Timothy 3:15, it tells us the house of God is the church of the living God and the pillar and ground of the truth. Colossians

1:18 states, "And he is the head of the body, the church" from which all the body is nourished (Colossians 2:19). The Bible also says that Jesus is the builder of His church (Matthew 16:18) and that, in fact, He owns the church (Ephesians 1:14). Would a mere human "Christ" own or control the church?

Careful consideration of the above Scriptures alone should be enough to answer that question. Moses, traditionally recognized as the greatest of all Old Testament figures, is a servant. Jesus Christ, the builder, created God's house. Only as God could He have done that!

Now, as we investigate the Scriptures further, we learn that Jesus created more than God's house—He created *all* things.

Christ is the architect (builder) of all things (Colossians 1:15-17) and is the head of the house, the body of Christ; therefore He is God. He also went to Heaven to prepare a place for the people of His household (John 14:2-3; Ephesians 2:19) that where He is we may be also.

Speaking of the Word who is Jesus Christ (e.g., John 1:14), the apostle John says:

> The same was in the beginning with God. All things were made by him; and without him was not any thing made that was made. (John 1:2-3)

John 1:10 states that "the world was made by him, and the world knew him not." God could not have made the worlds through the Son, as it states in Hebrews 1:2, if the Son did not exist prior to creation. One must exist before all things; otherwise he is one of the things created.

It is God who created all things. Christ is the architect (builder) of all things; therefore, He is God:

> [F]or by him [Jesus Christ] were all things created,
> that are in heaven, and that are in earth, visible and
> invisible, whether they be thrones, or dominions,
> or principalities, or powers: all things were created
> by him, and for him: And he is before all things,
> and by him all things consist. (Colossians 1:16-17)

And in Revelation 4:11, it explains that in Heaven, the saints say:

> Thou art worthy, O Lord, to receive glory and
> honour and power: for thou hast created all things,
> and for thy pleasure they are and were created.

What's more, in the entire first chapter of Hebrews, the Father proclaims Christ as the creator.

Some try to use the word "firstborn" to show that Jesus was created. The Greek word for firstborn (or first begotten) (*prototokos*) is found nine times in the New Testament. It means first in rank, an heir, to have preeminence in position. It does not refer to origin. The other Greek word for created is *protoktisis*, which is *not* used for Christ. Revelation 1:5 states:

> . . . and from Jesus Christ, who is the faithful
> witness, and the first begotten of the dead, and
> the prince of the kings of the earth.

Both Colossians 1:15 and Revelation 1:5 use this term for "firstborn," and the meaning is clarified by its context, in that He is the first one risen from the dead eternally. Christ was not the first raised from the dead, but He was the first raised to eternal life in the body, which gives Him headship over the human race, showing Him to be the heir of all things, and having preeminence.

And we mustn't forget what Revelation 3:14 reveals about Jesus Christ:

> These things saith the Amen, the faithful and true witness, the beginning of the creation of God.

Jehovah's Witnesses use this verse to attempt to prove Christ is the first to be created by God. However, the Greek word for beginning (*arche*) means that He is the source, the architect of creation; it actually proves the exact opposite of what cultists say. If one takes this position of the Son being created, then the Alpha and Omega (the *beginning* and the end) called "the Almighty" also had a beginning, for the same word is used (Revelation 1:8; 21:6, 22:13).

Scripture refers to the Son as the Word (*Logos*). He was in the beginning with God (John 1:2), this One who is called "the Word," who spoke in Genesis, and brought all things into existence. Speaking of Jesus, Hebrews1:3 says:

> . . . who being the brightness of his glory, and the express image of his person, and upholding all things by the word of his power.

The God who spoke things into existence is the God who continues to keep the universe in running order under His authority "upholding all things by the word of his power" (Hebrews 1:3).

8

JESUS, THE CREATOR —NOT THE BROTHER OF ANGELS

◆

The Book of Hebrews begins by telling us that God "hath in these last days spoken unto us by his Son, whom he hath appointed heir of all things, by whom also he made the worlds" (Hebrews 1:2). This agrees with what the apostle states in John 1:3: "All things were made by him; and without him was not any thing made that was made."

Athanasius (296-373) had used Hebrews 1:1-4 in his controversy with Arius who claimed Jesus was created. Athanasius used the verses to prove that the Son did not have a beginning, and His true essential nature was God.

Speaking of Jesus, Hebrews1:3 says:

> Who being the *brightness of his glory,* and the *express image* of his person, and upholding all things by the word of his power. (emphasis added)

The God who spoke things into existence as recorded in Genesis is the God who continues to keep the universe in running order.

No mere man can be "the brightness of His glory." Recall the revelation of Jesus' deity on the Mount of Transfiguration. He reveals His glory to His three disciples showing who He really is, as a brilliant white light exuded from within His body. Transfigured is the word *metamorphoo,* meaning a change of appearance. He was transfigured before them (Matthew 17:2). His face shone like the sun, and His clothes became as white as the light (also see Mark 9:1-10 and Luke 9:29-36) where the glory of the Father also descended upon the mountain, and the Voice spoke from the cloud, saying, "This is my beloved Son, in whom I am well pleased; hear ye him" (Matthew 17:1-6).

Looking again at Hebrews 1:3, according to *Strong's Exhaustive Concordance,* the word "image" in the Greek is:

> A graver (the tool or the person), i.e. (by implication) engraving (["character," the figure stamped, i.e. an exact copy or [figuratively] representation)—express image.

The writer, inspired by the Holy Spirit, is conveying that "the image" is the exact expression of the invisible God; that is what was made known to man by the Son. He was like His Father who remained invisible in every respect.

Now, what about the claim (of some cults) that Jesus was and is an angel. Again, the Book of Hebrews provides further insight into Jesus' true identity:

> . . . being made so much better than the angels, as
> he hath by inheritance obtained a more excellent
> name than they. (Hebrews 1:4)

How did He become better? By His exaltation after the resurrection, He returned to His former position in Heaven with a body (1 Timothy 2:5). He was already better in nature than the angels before His incarnation, being deity, the very One who created all the angels, and being made in the flesh a little lower than the angels, He experienced death on the Cross. But God the Father has exalted Him to His rightful position. As the Scripture states:

> For unto which of the angels said he at any time,
> Thou art my Son, this day have I begotten thee?
> (Hebrews 1:5)

Here the writer is proclaiming the Son as superior to all the angels. Angels as a species are called sons of God collectively, plural, but to no single angel is ascribed: "My Son" or begotten of God. While the angels are a great creation of God, the Son is said to be far better and unique. Why? Because the Son of God shares the same nature as His Father!

> And again, when he bringeth in the first begotten
> into the world, he saith, And let all the angels of
> God worship him. (Hebrews 1:6)

The Father brought the Son into the world *again* by the resurrection. Thus, Jesus is called "the first begotten of the dead" (Revelation 1:5), the first raised unto eternal life in the body, and in Colossians, it says that Jesus is "the firstborn from the dead; that in all things He might have the preeminence" (Colossians 1:18). He is "declared to be the Son of God with power, according to the spirit of holiness, by the resurrection from the dead" (Romans 1:4). Christ did not become God's Son for the first time at the resurrection, He *is* the Son, eternally. The Father proclaimed Him the Son of God "with power" to all people for all time by the resurrection. In 1 Corinthians 15:20, Paul, referring to Jesus' resurrection, identifies Jesus as "the firstfruits of them that slept." This means that another resurrection awaits "they that are Christ's at his coming" (1 Corinthians 15:23).

The Father tells all the angels to worship the Son. Do they worship His humanity, or do they worship God, the eternal Son? This shows that the Son is to be worshiped in the same way the Father is by His creatures. The only way angels can worship the Son is if they are subordinate to Him. Jesus said:

> That all men should honour the Son, even as they honour the Father. He that honoureth not the Son honoureth not the Father which hath sent him. (John 5:23)

Does the Father command us to give the same honor to a human that we are to give the Father who is God? Certainly not! Jesus is more than a man, more than the angels. To worship any creature except God is forbidden, yet here (Hebrews 1:6) we have God the Father telling the angels to worship the Son—which means He cannot be an angel or a mere man. Otherwise, the Father would be promoting idolatry!

This should shut down any thought entertained that Jesus is an angel (as the Jehovah's Witnesses and other cults claim). Again, in the Book of Hebrews, it further states:

> For unto the angels hath he *not* put in subjection the world to come, whereof we speak [but] Thou hast put all things in subjection under his [Jesus'] feet. (Hebrews 2:5,8; emphasis added)

In other words, the world will not be in subjection to angels, but it will be subject to Jesus. Logic then dictates that Jesus cannot possibly be an angel. God Himself has said so. In the first chapter of Hebrews, God the Father says:

> But unto the Son he saith, Thy throne, O God, is for ever and ever: a sceptre of righteousness is the sceptre of thy kingdom. (Hebrews 1:8)

This quote repeats what is stated in Psalm 45:6 and is an emphatic statement declaring the Son (Jesus) to be God. Not only this, but it refers to an eternal throne—something that can only belong to God (since only God was never created). Again the Father speaking of the Son proclaims:

> And, Thou, Lord, in the beginning hast laid the foundation of the earth; and the heavens are the works of thine hands. (Hebrews 1:10)

This declaration is confirmed by John 1:3; Hebrews 1:2, and Colossians 1:15-17.

The Father addresses the Son as eternal, the Creator of all things, and calls the Son Lord (Yahweh) and says He was present as the architect who began creation of both the heaven and the earth, (both of which were created by God, (Genesis 1:1).

In Isaiah 48:13, the prophet states:

> Mine hand also hath laid the foundation of the earth, and my right hand hath spanned the heavens: when I call unto them, they stand up together.

In Judaism, the right hand of God is symbolic of the Messiah.

The following Old Testament verses speak of God while attributing the same qualities to the Son:

> Of old hast thou [referring to the Son] laid the foundation of the earth: and the heavens are the work of thy hands. They shall perish, but thou shalt endure: yea, all of them shall wax old like a garment; as a vesture shalt thou change them, and they shall be changed: But thou art the same, and thy years shall have no end. (Psalm 102:25-27)

It is clear the writer's intent is to apply this passage to the Lord Jesus to prove conclusively that He is greater than the angels; He is, in fact, Deity. A plain reading of the above verses could lead only to the conclusion that the one being addressed is God. The same is evident in Hebrews 1:10.

Therefore, the Son is just as real and present before the creation of the world as the Father is. He is, as the Father says, the Creator.

> And as a vesture shalt thou fold them up, and they
> shall be changed: but thou art the same, and thy
> years shall not fail. (Hebrews 1:12)

Malachi 3:6 says, "For I am the LORD, I change not." Only God the Creator does not change. The Father addresses the Son as eternal and immutable with His assertion that "they will perish, you will remain."

We know from Scripture that the Father is eternal (James1:17). This is never disputed by anti-Trinitarians since it is essential for God to possess an eternal nature in order to create all things. What they dispute is that the Son is also eternal. Speaking of Jesus in prophecy, Micah 5:2 says, "[W]hose goings forth have been from of old, from everlasting [from eternity]." And in Hebrews 13:8, it says, "Jesus Christ the same yesterday, and to day, and for ever" meaning that His nature is unchangeable.

In Hebrews 1:13, the writer of the epistle, quoting Psalm 110:1 says:

> But to which of the angels said he at any time,
> Sit on my right hand, until I make thine enemies
> thy footstool?

In Luke 22:67, 69, the Pharisees pressed Jesus with their demands of "Art thou the Christ? tell us" (Luke 22:67). To which Jesus answered:

> Hereafter shall the Son of man sit on the right
> hand of the power of God.

Then they all said, "Art thou then the Son of God?" (v. 70). The Pharisees understood the phrase "the Son of man" which was from Daniel 7:13, and the use of the phrase "right hand of the power of God," which was a messianic reference (Acts 5:31).

In Matthew 26:63, the high priest said to Jesus, "I adjure thee [put under oath] by the living God, that thou tell us whether thou be the Christ, the Son of God."

Jesus said to him:

> Thou hast said: nevertheless I say unto you,
> Hereafter shall ye see the Son of man sitting on
> the right hand of power, and coming in the clouds
> of heaven. (v. 64)

In Daniel's vision, he describes seeing the Son of man coming with the clouds of Heaven (Daniel 7:13).

First Peter 3:22 states that He is "on the right hand of God; angels and authorities and powers being made subject unto him."

If Jesus Christ were only a man, then the ruling of the universe is now in mere human hands. Likewise, if Jesus were only an angel, then He would be a created being—not the pre-existent Creator of the universe—ruling as God with the Father. He is contrasted to the angels, but He is superior to them: "unto which of the angels said he at any time, Thou art my Son" or "to which of the angels said he at any time, Sit on my right hand, until I make thine enemies thy footstool?" The answer is not one.

9

THREE PERSONS VERSUS THREE MANIFESTATIONS

◆

Can the Father, the Son and the Comforter be three manifestations rather than three persons?

When speaking of "manifestations" in the Old Testament, God's glory physically appeared to be seen by man in various forms such as fire, light, a cloud, and deep darkness. In the era of the early church, the Oneness heresy claimed that the one God appeared as different manifestations in sequential order in different ages. Oneness adherents did this because they recognized the Father, Son, and Holy Spirit as personal. The main promoter, Praxeas, taught that the Father and the Son were one identical person and that the Father became man. By the third century, Sabellius, who resided in Rome, tried to iron out any kinks. According to his view, the Father, Son, and Holy Spirit are all one and the same. The one God manifests Himself in three different ways, and these do not have a simultaneous existence.

Modern Oneness considers the Son to be human, and what makes Him God in the flesh is the Father dwelling in Him, which is the Spirit. Another prevalent Oneness view today is that the three manifestations of the one God—Father, Son, and Holy Ghost—are all Jesus. In the Bible (especially Isaiah), God speaks of Himself in the plural, which is not applicable when there is one manifestation at a time:

[A]nd who will go for us ? (Isaiah 6:8)

[F]rom the time that it was, there am I: and now the Lord God, and his Spirit, hath sent me [describing three]. (Isaiah 48:16)

Throughout Scripture, examples can be found of two or three present at the same time, speaking and conversing (as in John 12:28).

John 14:16 states:

And I will pray the Father, and he shall give you another Comforter, that he may abide with you for ever.

Jesus considered the Holy Spirit as another like Himself but *other* than Himself, just as He thought of the Father as another. Here are all three—Jesus, the Father, and *another* Comforter. In Greek, *allos paracletos* means another of the same kind, like Jesus the Son. The word allos "another" is used in John's gospel for personal subjects, showing distinction and contrast. He is not sending an office or a different

THE TRINITY

manifestation of Himself. He is a person, and He is sending another person.

Although Spirit is neutral in the Greek language, Paul uses the masculine pronoun *he* in reference to the Spirit (John 14:16; 15:26; 16:8, 13) giving Him separate personal identity from the Son and the Father. The Holy Spirit is portrayed as a personal being with a self-identity different from both the Father and the Son. John does the same in distinguishing Jesus as a separate person from the Father when he tells us in John 1:1, "[T]he Word was with God, and the Word was God." Verses 2 and 3 say, "The same [Greek pronoun for "he"] was in the beginning with God. All things were made by him." The Bible calls the Word a Him who is a person existing at the same time as the other. If Jesus were all three manifestations—Father, Son, and Holy Spirit—then God acts in roles, modes, offices, and manifestations—anything but three persons. This would make the New Testament inconsistent and contradictory in its words and meanings. The roles are like clothes one wears for different occasions to fulfill an activity. From this comes the denial of an eternal Son, and with that an eternal Father because they are only temporary roles and are dispensed with after they are used by the one "person" who is God. They cease to exist.

What is at stake here is the authenticity of God's revelation of who He actually is. How can one know or understand who God is if He constantly has temporary roles that change back and forth indiscriminately from one to the other? Since God is presented as eternal in His nature, unchanging, He reveals Himself as who He is, not as who He is not! If God were always a manifestation, then He changes. Furthermore, if He were changing into different roles (which we identify as persons), God is no longer the eternal "I Am" but the eternal "I was"; He was the Father, now He's the Son, next He is the Holy Spirit, and next He will be . . . you can fill in the blank with any one of His roles, titles, and offices. If the Father changes to something else, then neither the Son or the Father are eternal or self-existent in their identity.

For example in Hebrews 1:8-12, God the Father is quoted as speaking of the Son:

> But unto the Son he saith . . . And, Thou, Lord, in the beginning hast laid the foundation of the earth; and the heavens are the works of thine hands: They shall perish; but thou remainest; and they all shall wax old as doth a garment; and as a vesture shalt thou fold them up, and they shall be changed: but thou art the same, and thy years shall not fail.

This affirms Malachi 3:6, which says, "For I am the Lord, I change not."

God can't be revealed in three persons unless in truthfulness that is who He is permanently from everlasting to everlasting (Psalm 106:48). Because He has an eternal (infinite) nature, He never comes into or out of existence, nor changes. Otherwise, He would have a beginning. It also means He would have an end, changing from one mode to another. The former manifestation is then non-existent. The Bible actually portrays three persons as simultaneously existing. There was never a time when the three were not one God.

On two occasions, the Father speaks from Heaven in a literal, audible voice calling Jesus His Son: at the

Transfiguration (Matthew 17:5; Mark 9:7; and Luke 9:35) and at Jesus' baptism (Matthew 3:17) where a voice from Heaven speaks, "This is my beloved Son, in whom I am well pleased." The one who calls another His Son identifies Himself as the Father. Notice from where the voice comes each time—Heaven. (The cloud is a visible manifestation of God's glory. 2 Peter 1:17 tells us the voice was from Heaven.) Notice the Father says, Hear Him!" Roles, manifestations do not speak to another role—persons do! At the very least, one has to concede that three persons are simultaneously existing.

At Jesus' baptism, we see two actual persons; one is communicating with a third person coming from Heaven resting upon Him. Intercommunication requires more than one mind and person. Minds show personalities of different consciousness. We see a personal communication of one to another before the incarnation, during, and afterward.

If there is a time they disappear to reappear as a different person, then neither the Father nor the Spirit are eternal, which proves they are not the God of the Bible who is eternal, indivisible, and unquantifiable, who cannot change.

To add to the confusion, one would have to ask, which one is not a manifestation? Does a manifestation (or a role) send another manifestation? Did a manifestation (the Father) send the Son? Did Jesus teach us to pray to a manifestation called the Father in Heaven while He was on Earth? And if you can only have one manifestation be a person at a time, how can Jesus even communicate with the Father or have the Holy Spirit descend on Him visibly as a dove?

The Oneness view of God denies the distinctions are real, saying they are only roles or offices God uses for His different functions. Only persons portray different identities. The Father and the Holy Spirit are never called Jesus, only the Son, nor do we see Jesus called the Father or the Comforter called Jesus. Over fifty times, Jesus the Son and the Father are mentioned in the same verse, showing distinction.

WHY THESE THREE ARE NOT MANIFESTATIONS BUT PERSONS

First Timothy 3:16 says it was God that was manifested in the flesh, but except for the context, it does not tell us who. Nowhere does it say the Father was manifested in the flesh. The only time a specific person of God is mentioned as being manifested is in 1 John 3:8, "For this purpose the Son of God was manifested, that he might destroy the works of the devil." The Greek word for manifest is *emphanizo* meaning: 1) to manifest, to exhibit, to view; and 2) to show oneself; to appear. Try to find the word manifest in the Bible for all three persons of the Trinity; it's not there.

All three were not manifested in the flesh. The "Son of God" was manifested in the flesh; it's singular, not plural. This is not a small difference of interpretation; this is *the* point of contention.

John 1:18 states:

> No man hath seen God at any time; the only begotten Son, which is in the bosom of the Father, he hath declared him.

When was the Son with the Father in this manner? Before He was incarnated. And He, as a person, is revealing another person to us, the Father.

WHY THEY ARE CALLED PERSONS

The plain sense of Scripture indicates three distinct identities. Throughout the Scriptures, God's persons are seen as both agent and object, exhibiting intelligence and consciousness showing emotion and relationship. The divine nature is one, which includes plurality that is inseparable—not dividing the divine Essence; so there must be a plurality of persons.

A mediator, redeemer, or savior are terms that apply to a role or a position of a particular person. When one speaks of a father or son, that is describing a person.

Oneness teaches the Father and Son are only roles of a single person, who is God. Biblically, the terms of the Son and Father are titles that belong to two different personalities. *The Son* is a title of a person. Does one know of any sons who are not persons? *The Father* is a title of a person. Does one know of any fathers who are not persons?

The Father and Son are seen communicating; this means they are persons, not manifestations. The Bible *never* says there is only one person in the Godhead, nor does it describe them as temporal, appearing one at a time, changing back to each other.

Scripture is clear in its presentation that they all exist *simultaneously,* and they are all eternal. The Father is eternal (James 1:17). The Son is eternal (Hebrews 13:8; Micah 5:2). The Holy Spirit is eternal (Hebrews 9:14; John 4:24). The

Father was involved in the creation (Ephesians 3:14-15; Malachi 2:10). The Son was involved in the creation (John 1:3; Hebrews 1:2; and Colossians 1:16). The Holy Spirit was involved in the creation (Genesis 1:2; Psalm 104:30; Job 26:13; and Job 33:4). So all three and no more than three are all present—simultaneous and active.

Describing the unity of persons who are eternal and infinite has its difficulties in our language. Deity is not the same type of unity we would use to describe someone in the finite world. There are no corresponding analogies with something finite and created. We can only apprehend what God has said of Himself. To do this, we must take all of the Scripture and not compartmentalize portions we cannot understand.

10

THE SON WITH THE FATHER

———◆———

In John 1:1, John refers to the creation account of Genesis using the same words as in Genesis 1:1: "In the beginning." He also introduces the "Word" (logos) who was "with God" (present in the beginning) and who "was God." The word "with" couples two pronouns; it expresses a union and therefore more than one. John 1:1 is describing an actual conscious existence of the Son (the word) at the Father's side (*para soi*). In John 17:5, the Son asks the Father, "glorify Me together with Yourself, with the glory which I had *with Thee* [para soi] before the world was." He is asking for what He had previously in Heaven to be restored. This shows us two important points: first, He pre-existed as a distinct person from the Father by being *with* the Father, and second, He *shared* in the same glory before the world began.

John 1:18 further develops this idea in that the "Word" is now identified as "the only begotten Son, which is in the bosom of the Father." Greek scholar A. T. Robertson translates the literal rendering of the language as, "by the side of thyself" thereby designating a unity of the two distinct persons who are equal in essence and share the same glory. The only way the Son can share in the same glory as the Father is if He were God, for the Lord has said, "[M]y glory will I not give to another (Isaiah 42:8).

Genesis 1:1 tells us the first things created were the heavens and the earth. If Jesus shared the glory with the Father prior to this time (John 1:3), then He pre-existed as God—for only God existed before anything was created. Therefore, it is impossible for Him to have been a creature. He became a creature through the virgin birth by taking on human flesh to house His deity (Micah 5:2).

11

JESUS IS *THE* WORD, NOT *A* WORD

---◆---

> In the beginning was the Word, and the Word was with God, and the Word was God. (John 1:1)

The Greek word *logos* (rendered here as "Word") does not mean Jesus is a word spoken. The word logos is not something spoken as an impersonal "it." The word was not an idea, a thought, or an expression. English Bible scholar W. E. Vine states:

> John's use of the word logos is entirely to be distinguished from the use made of it by Philo of Alexandria and his school of philosophy in the second century B.C. With them the logos was an impersonal idea, conveying the thoughts of God.[5]

The term logos is applied to Christ in John 1:1,14, in Revelation 19:13, and in the possible use of a personification of "the Word of God" in Hebrews 4:12. John uses "eternal life" (which was with the Father) as a similar metaphor in 1 John 1:2. The logos is portrayed as a pre-existent eternal being. The logos was used by the Greeks to denote the creative force, as well as logic and reason. John 1:1 states, "the Word was God" thereby explaining that the Word is a personal eternal person in God's being. John's use of the imperfect tense in the Greek shows continuous duration of existence in the past and continuing into the future. If the "Word" is something issuing forth as speech and then becoming human, then it is not deity. It is no more than any other created thing or creature. How could a word spoken be God? For the Word to be interpreted as something God spoke would mean that God is not an eternal personal being. The Bible says the Word is a person, not that the person is the word or speech. We find that this Word is another title representing the Son of God, who has the same nature as the Father. He is called the Word because He is the active cause of the world. It is He who spoke things into existence. He is also the personification of the wisdom of God in the Old Testament. Christ is called the Word and is the Truth. God communicated to man in ancient times by His Word through the prophets, but now has communicated to us directly through His Son, who became a man. This Word who made all things as the work of His own hands became His own workmanship.

Jesus stated:

> Verily, verily, I say unto you, he that heareth my word, and believeth on him that sent me, hath everlasting life. (John 5:24)

He also said that the words He speaks are His (Mark 13:31; Luke 9:26; and John 5:47) and are the Father's (John 14:24). In John 8:54-55, Jesus says He always keeps the Father's word. It is the words of *both* which prove two persons exist. Psalm 138:2 says:

> [F]or thou hast magnified thy word above all thy name.

The same John who wrote the gospel writes in Revelation 19:13:

> And he was clothed with a vesture dipped in blood: and his name is called The Word of God.

Who is the He? His name is called The Word of God, not He is a word. The Word is a person; this same person is the Son of God in Revelation 2:18. In Hebrews 1:2, it states that God made the worlds through the Son. If we parallel Revelation 19:13 and Isaiah 9:6, one of the Son's names will be called the mighty God.

But thou, Bethlehem Ephratah, though thou be little among the thousands of Judah, yet out of thee shall he come forth unto me that is to be ruler in Israel; whose goings forth have been from of old, from everlasting. (Micah 5:2)

12

A SON IS GIVEN

———◆———

Then spake Jesus again unto them, saying, "I am the light of the world: he that followeth me shall not walk in darkness, but shall have the light of life." (John 8:12)

Isaiah 9:6 tells us a child would be born, referring to Christ's birth, which united His deity with His humanity. It also says that a Son would be given, referring to His original nature as the Son in His pre-existence. He is sent from Heaven as the Son (His pre-existent condition) (John 3:16; 6:39; 12:49), but came as a child, born of a woman whom Isaiah 7:14 identifies as a virgin—a birth without man's seed, a supernatural birth. This is why He is termed the last Adam, because He had no previous generation.

The first man is of the earth, earthy: the second man is the Lord from heaven. (1 Corinthians 15:47)

Both Adam and Jesus were given directly by God with no pro-creative act; both had supernatural births. Both were created without sin, but only one, the last Adam, lived a sinless life and was able to redeem us from our sin—His was a life-giving Spirit. The first Adam was of Earth; the last Adam was the Son of God (the Lord) who came from Heaven to restore our relationship with God.

Isaiah 9:6 also calls this Child/Son divine names, such as "Wonderful, Counsellor, The mighty God, The everlasting Father, The Prince of Peace." This verse also reveals that He has a government and a kingdom without end.

Oneness Pentecostals use "everlasting Father" in Isaiah 9:6 to attempt to prove that Jesus is actually the Father, who became the Son. But the Hebrew word for Father (*Ab*) is not used here in the begetting sense; rather the connective word for Father (*Abi*) is used with the word for eternal or everlasting (*Ad*). Hence, we have the compound word construction Abi-Ad (literally "Father of eternity") which we know from the context of Isaiah 9:6 refers to the "son" who is given. The use of the word construction Abi-Ad, however, cannot be referring to a created Christ, but One who always existed as God—both eternal and the source of all creation.

From Isaiah 9:6, we learn that Jesus existed from eternity past. Therefore, at the incarnation, He as the Son, a distinct person in the Trinity, was born as a human.

13

"ONLY BEGOTTEN," "MONOGENES"

———◆———

"Only Begotten" is not a biological term, nor does it mean Jesus is God's only born Son. It actually means that Jesus is God's one and only eternal Son. This terminology is exclusive to the Gospel of John. He applies it five times to the Savior.

John 3:16 says, God "gave his only begotten Son" so we may have everlasting life. The Greek word for "only begotten" is *monogenes*, and it is formed by two separate words. Mono means "single" or "one" and can be interpreted as meaning "sole" or "lone" as in the idea of there being one God (monotheism). Genes on its own carries the meaning of "begotten" or "offspring" or progeny. However, when the two words are combined, it means uniquely one of a kind, no other like Him, the only one generated. As He is the unique Son uncreated but generated (i.e., taking on human form while remaining fully God), He is the only example of this category—God's unique representative as the only God/man. What it does *not* mean is that He is a literal offspring having a beginning, when in fact He is eternally existent as the Son along with the Father.

John 1:14 explains:

> And the Word was made [became] flesh, and dwelt among us, (and we beheld his glory, the glory as of the only begotten of the Father).

Regarding the phrase "was made flesh," "became" in Greek is *ginomai*, which means "to cause or become what it was not." John began his Gospel (John 1:1) with the proof that the Word was equal with God and *is* God. In verse 14, this Word became flesh, indicating that He who had pre-existence became man. Scripture declares in 1 Timothy 3:16: "God was manifest in the flesh." This also goes together with Jesus' prayer of restoration in that He asks to be glorified with the glory He previously had with the Father (John 17:5).

The principle of begetting in the natural world was instituted at creation, in which everything produces after its own kind. An apple tree will produce apples, an orange tree produces oranges, a dog will produce a dog, and a human will produce a human. There are no natural exceptions. Anti-Trinitarians are hard-pressed to interpret "begotten" in a literal sense, claiming that the person of Jesus was begotten, meaning to them that He had a beginning. The reasoning goes that since each begets after its own kind, if Christ is begotten, and this means He is flesh (a human son), then the Father who begot Him is also flesh (human). This obviously is not true, since Scripture tells us that God is Spirit. So, while it is true that the Son possesses the same nature and attributes as the Father, it is false to presume that the Father must be in the flesh because Jesus came in the flesh. The only way out of this tremendous flaw in anti-Trinitarian theology is to abandon this interpretation of "literally begotten." For if the Holy Spirit begat flesh, then He, too, is flesh. This term must therefore have another meaning than the normal interpretation of literally begotten, as in "offspring."

Regarding the name Son, theologian Louis Berkhof states:

> He is spoken of as the Son of God from a pre-incarnation standpoint, for instance, in John 1:14, 18; Galatians 4:4, He is called the "only begotten" Son of God or of the Father, a term that would not apply to Him if He were the Son of God only in an official or in an ethical sense.[6]

A. T. Robertson, on John 1:18, says:

> [T]he correct text [is] "God only begotten" (theos . . . monogenees). So he is "God only begotten.". . . The eternal relation of the Son with the Father.[7]

John 1:18, which says, "the only begotten Son, which is in the bosom of the Father," explains that the Son has an exclusive relation to the Father with an intimate and full knowledge of God that no one else has. This idea is echoed in Jesus' own words in Matthew 11:27 when He states, "[N]either knoweth any man the Father, save the Son."

Charles Hodge, the nineteenth century Princeton theologian wrote:

The Council [of Nicea] declared that our Lord is the Eternal Son of God i.e., that He is from eternity the Son of God. This of course involves the denial that He became the Son of God in time; and, consequently, that the primary and essential reason for His being called Son is not His miraculous birth, nor his incarnation, nor His resurrection, nor His exaltation to the right hand of God. The Council decided that the word Son as applied to Christ, is not a term of office but of nature; that it expresses the relationship which the Second Person in the Trinity from eternity bears to the First Person, and that the relationship thus indicated is sameness of nature, so that sonship, in the case of Christ, includes equality with God. In other words, God was in such a sense his Father that He was equal with God. And consequently every time the Scriptures call Jesus the Son of God, they assert his true and proper divinity.[8]

Paul applies the word "begotten" to Jesus after the resurrection:

God hath fulfilled the same unto us their children, in that he hath raised up Jesus again; as it is also written in the second psalm, Thou art my Son, this day have I begotten thee. (Acts 13:33)

This "begotten" proves it does not mean a birth but something different. Jesus did not become the Son because of the resurrection. As Hebrews 1:5-6 states:

> For unto which of the angels said he at any time,
> Thou art my Son, this day have I begotten thee?
> And again, I will be to him a Father, and he shall
> be to me a Son? And again, when he bringeth in
> the firstbegotten into the world, he saith, And let
> all the angels of God worship him.

God brought Jesus into the world again by the resurrection.

The above passage in Hebrews asks a rhetorical question in posing the thought: To what angel would the Father ever say, "Thou art my Son . . ." and "let all the angels of God worship him"? Clearly, with statements from the Father like these, Jesus could not possibly be a mere angel, so He too must be God, uniquely God with the Father. These events all share in common a decree announcing publicly who Jesus is, openly declaring Him to be the Son of God. Each time it was a specific revelation to certain people. It was not that on a certain day He became the Son, but that He was declared the Son on each separate day. This declaration of Father and Son are terms describing a relationship by nature, not by origination.

The Father declares the fact that the Son is indeed Lord. He is the firstborn from the dead unto eternal life in the body (Colossians 1:18; Revelation 1:5). And in Romans 1:4 Paul states:

> . . . and declared to be the Son of God with
> power, according to the spirit of holiness, by the
> resurrection from the dead.

Christ did not become God's Son for the first time by the resurrection; He already was the Son. The Father proclaimed this "with power" to all people for all time by the renewing of life. By the resurrection, Jesus is proven to be the "only begotten Son" the only man raised in a body unto eternal life, as "the firstfruits of them that slept" (1 Corinthians 15:20). We who believe will be raised at our resurrection after his likeness and will have incorruptible eternal physical bodies.

After the resurrection, Jesus pointed to His Father, saying, "All power is given unto me in heaven and in earth" (Matthew 28:18). Notice it says all power (meaning authority) is given to Him in Heaven and Earth, which means He rules in both places. Jesus was exalted to His former position; He then commissions the apostles to preach and baptize in His name.

14

THE PRE-EXISTENT SON
WHO BECAME MAN

———————◆———————

At the baptism of Christ, the voice of the Father spoke
from Heaven, saying:

> This is my beloved Son, in whom I am well
> pleased. (Matthew 3:17)

He did not say that Jesus had become His Son. The
Holy Spirit came down from the Father in Heaven and put
His seal of approval on the Son by resting on Him.

Jesus becoming the Son at His birth or at His baptism
is what is called "adoptionism," a heresy in the early church.
According to the Scriptures, Christ did not become the Son
in actual time—not by His birth, His baptism, or His resurrection. Jesus did not *become* God's Son at any given time.
This is a timeless declaration of Jesus being the Son from all
eternity. The decree declared by the Father is that Jesus is the
Father's *only* Son *from* eternity. We can see this demonstrated

by the several times Jesus is identified as the Son by the Father in an audible voice from Heaven. It was not just Jesus who said He was the Son; the Father spoke from Heaven three times saying, "this is my beloved Son" and continually testified of Him as the Son throughout His ministry.

Jesus' baptism has all three persons involved witnessing Jesus as the Son. However, Jesus stated:

> But I receive not testimony from man [referring to John, the Baptist] . . . But I have greater witness than that of John. (John 5:34, 36)

Who is the greater witness? His Father, of course. Just as John was a witness, so the Father in Heaven is another person witnessing of the Son on Earth.

Jesus answers His detractors in John 8:16-18:

> And yet if I judge, my judgment is true: for I am not alone, but I and the Father that sent me. It is also written in your law, that the testimony of two men is true. I am one that bear witness of myself, and the Father that sent me beareth witness of me.

Jesus' purpose is to show that God the Father testifies who the Son actually is and from where He was sent. The Father is bearing witness of Jesus' deity. The Jewish system of law required two or more individuals to bear witness. God the Father's witness is of the Son sent from Heaven by Him. The Son's witness is revealing who He actually is—one with the Father. If this were not true, He would be deceiving us or lying, thereby breaking the law and sinning.

God sent the Holy Spirit in a physical manner to show from where the Son was sent (Heaven) and from where His approval comes (God the Father in Heaven). The Holy Spirit descends on Him in the likeness of a dove (in Luke's account, it says the Spirit came in bodily form). This causes the Father to speak audibly from Heaven:

> This is my beloved Son, in whom I am well pleased. (Matthew 3:17)

All three members of the one God are present and functioning together (see also Mark 1:9-11 and Luke 3:21-22). To further clarify this event in John 1:34, John the Baptist, in recalling what he witnessed at Christ's baptism testifies, "this is the Son of God."

At the transfiguration described in Matthew 17:5, Mark 9:7, and Luke 9:34-35, we read:

> [T]here was a cloud that overshadowed them: and a voice came out of the cloud, saying, This is my beloved Son: hear him. Mark 9:7)

This is God the Father testifying in the presence of three witnesses—Peter, James, and John—that Jesus is indeed the Son of God. Notice that the Father says to listen to Jesus. Is the Father pointing to Him as a human or as Deity? In 2 Peter 1:16-18, Peter recalls the voice that came from the Father in Heaven declaring Jesus to be His Son.

Jesus also spoke of the equality He had with the Father in the following two verses:

If I honour myself, my honour is nothing: it is my Father that honoureth me; of whom ye say, that he is your God. (John 8:54)

For the Father judgeth no man, but hath committed all judgment unto the Son: That all men should honour the Son, even as they honour the Father. He that honoureth not the Son honoureth not the Father which hath sent him. (John 5:22-23)

To prove Jesus was given authority to judge, He stated, "The hour is coming, and now is, when the dead shall hear the voice of the Son of God: and they that hear shall live" (John 5:25). He raised the dead during his ministry, and His will be the voice they hear in the resurrection.

15

THE SON SENT FROM HEAVEN BY THE FATHER

———————◆———————

Sacrifice and offering thou wouldest not, but a
body hast thou prepared me . . . Then said I, Lo,
I come (in the volume of the book it is written of
me,) to do thy will, O God. (Hebrews 10:5, 7)

If we look at the "me" who is referenced in this passage,
we see it is God the Son, who came in human flesh. This
obviously is not Jesus speaking to Himself, to prepare a body
for Himself so that He will do His own will. That kind of
rendering defies both logic and context. John 8:42 proceeds
in the same vein when Jesus said of Himself, "I proceeded
forth and came from God; neither came I of myself, but he
sent me." If Christ was sent by the Father and is deity, then
this makes two who are God. The "me" who came from
Heaven is deity, another person sent. When the apostle
Paul in Galatians 4:4 writes, "[B]ut when the fulness of the
time was come, God sent forth his Son" he is referring to an
event that took place at a certain point in time. According

to one Bible commentator, "The words 'sent forth' imply that the Son already existed in Heaven before He was sent." This means He preexisted, that He came from God; Mary, His earthly mother, was not His source for existence. His humanness came from Mary but not His deity. If one looks at how the word "sent" is applied to Christ, it's plain to see it involves two different persons—the one sending and the one sent. In John 16:28, Jesus makes this clear:

> I came forth from the Father, and am come into the world: again, I leave the world, and go to the Father.

Paul helps us identify from where He came:

> The first man is of the earth, earthy: the second man is the Lord from heaven. (1 Corinthians 15:47)

Paul makes an obvious distinction between the first man Adam who came from the earth and the one who descended to the earth from above to become man (see also John 3:13). The origin of the Son comes from above, showing us who the Son actually is.

All these statements show that His beginning is not on Earth. John 3:16-17 says that God gave His only begotten Son and that He sent his Son into the world. In fact, the Old Testament also explains that the Son was sent:

> Come ye near unto me, hear ye this; I have not spoken in secret from the beginning; from the

> time that it was, there am I: and now the Lord
> God, and his Spirit, hath sent me. (Isaiah 48:16)

If He was there from the beginning and He was sent by another, then He cannot be the same one who sent Him. In John 6:38, Jesus states:

> For I came down from heaven, not to do mine own
> will, but the will of him that sent me.

Hebrews 10:5-7 dovetails perfectly with this. He came from Heaven already as the Son. And we see also that Jesus made this clear when He said:

> And this is the Father's will which hath sent me,
> that of all which he hath given me I should lose
> nothing, but should raise it up again at the last
> day. (v. 39)

This was His purpose, to reveal God and to die for our sins. Repeatedly He emphasizes this:

> But I know him: for I am from him, and he hath
> sent me. (John 7:29)

> For the bread of God is he which cometh down
> from heaven, and giveth life unto the world.
> (John 6:33)

In typology, as the manna sustained Israel through the wilderness, Jesus is the bread of life for everyone.

He that cometh from above is above all: he that is of the earth is earthly, and speaketh of the earth: he that cometh from heaven is above all. (John 3:31)

I am the living bread which came down from heaven. (John 6:51)

And no man hath ascended up to heaven, but he that came down from heaven, even the Son of man which is in heaven. (John 3:13)

Jesus is pointing out that the one they are seeing came from above, not from Earth below.

What and if ye shall see the Son of man ascend up where he was before? (John 6:62)

And he said unto them, Ye are from beneath; I am from above: ye are of this world; I am not of this world. (John 8:23)

Since He is not a man or an angel coming from Heaven, who is He?

Not that any man hath seen the Father, save he which is of God, he hath seen the Father. (John 6:46)

Here Jesus indicates He is not just a man but that He has seen the Father. This is something no man can do! John 1:18 explains:

No man hath seen God at any time; the only
begotten Son, which is in the bosom of the Father,
he hath declared him.

Jesus is expressing His unique and special relationship
with the unseen God that no man can have.

The Son, who existed by the side of the Father, was
sent by the Father to Earth. This rules out Him being the
Father as some sects claim. In the Old Testament, the Son
was the messenger (Angel) of the Lord, the covenant maker
to Israel. In the New Testament, the Son becomes a human
being taking on the flesh of man through a virgin by the
Holy Spirit.

Romans 8:3 says:

God sending his own Son in the likeness of sinful
flesh.

The Son was sent from Heaven into our world; it does
not say the human Jesus became the Son. While there were
many prophets sent, such as John the Baptizer, their origin
was not from Heaven nor did they proceed from God or
see God. In Matthew 3:11, John the Baptist made that clear
when he said, speaking of Jesus:

[H]e that cometh after me is mightier than I,
whose shoes I am not worthy to bear.

16

PHILIPPIANS 2:5-8–
THE KENOSIS

———◆———

S peaking of Jesus in Philippians 2:6, the apostle Paul said, "who, being in the form of God, thought it not robbery to be equal with God." He continues with this idea in verse 7:

> . . . but made himself of no reputation, and took upon him the form of a servant, and was made in the likeness of men.

The form of God, His essence of being, is (uncreated) Spirit. The Greek word for form is *morphe*, meaning quality or the essential character that makes something what it is. Whatever the Father is in nature, so is the Son. Here Christ already existed in this nature and did not consider it to be theft to be equal with His Father who is God.

Form is a term that expresses the sum of those characterizing qualities which make a thing the precise thing that it is. *The International Standard Bible Encyclopedia* explains:

> Paul is not telling us here, then, what our Lord was once, but rather what He already was, or, better, what in His intrinsic nature He is.[10]

The word "being" is also essential to understanding this passage. In Greek, it is *huparcho*, a participle which means never stopped being (implying a prior existence). What it is telling us is the Son (Jesus Christ) stays the same in His nature. It is something that remains timeless, not pointing to any moment when Jesus "started" to exist in the form of God because Christ, the Son, has always been (subsisted) in the form of God. Because of this, He did not have to covet or strive for something He already possessed in eternity. Instead, He emptied Himself of what was rightfully His when He became man.

The word "equal" is also essential to understanding this passage's intent. The Greek word *isos* is in the neuter and is plural (i.e., equalities). This is where we get the word for an isosceles triangle with three equal sides. They are equal, making up an eternal symmetry of nature. Jesus' existence is equal to that of the Father—both persons are equal in nature.

First Timothy 3:16 tells us, "God was manifest in [appeared in] the flesh." First John 4:2 and 2 John 1:7 both communicate the same meaning—He came in the flesh.

This incarnation (becoming man) is what is called the "emptying" of Christ, in the Greek *eke-nosen* (meaning "empty or vacate" *kenou*, to empty Himself). In becoming a man, something changed since He was not in a servant role to the Father before He became man. This was a change of position, not a change in nature. He, as God, cannot empty Himself of His essential nature since unchangeableness is part of being God (Malachi 3:6). All His attributes are eternal, so He could not eliminate any; He could, however, put aside His privileges in using them independently as He entered time and space when He became a man and lived a life in submission to the Father.

In theology, this event is called the *hypostatic union*, in which undiminished deity and full humanity are united in one person (forever). He is the only God/man with two distinct and different natures, side-by-side residing in one person. These natures were kept distinct without mingling; there was no transferring of one nature to the other. In His humanity, He could be weak, hungry, and tired, requiring all the necessities inherent in humanity. There was still an organic union where His deity felt what His humanity did, since He was one person. In His deity, He had the ability to know all things and to do anything the Father instructed Him to do.

When someone becomes a slave, he does not give up his skills, but submits to another in a higher position. This is why, at that time, Jesus said, "[M]y Father is greater than I" (John 14:28). Positionally, He was a servant until after the resurrection, when He entered again into His former position of glory with the Father.

It is not the humanity that was lowered, for it says in Philippians 2:7:

> . . . but made himself of no reputation [the kenosis], and took upon him the form of a servant, and was made in the likeness of men.

Notice that the one Paul is describing first existed in the nature of God (v. 6) and then put aside His reputation when taking on the form (nature) of another, the form of a servant, being made a man. The phraseology "the form of a servant" is identical in its content to "the form of God." As the Son, He voluntarily laid aside the use of His divine attributes and privileges and entered the world of human existence, taking on the role of a servant by adding a human nature to His deity. He did not exchange His deity for humanity, but He took on an additional nature—one of humanity. So it wasn't as much a subtraction as it was an addition. "Remaining what He was, He became what He was not."[12] Becoming a human being became His experience. He came as a servant, submitting Himself to the Father's will, which He fulfilled perfectly. Whatever was laid aside in the emptying, or *kenosis,* was not permanent because He took it up again at the resurrection. He continued to serve others, and even after His resurrection, He served His disciples by starting a fire and cooking fish for them.

> [B]eing found in fashion as a man, he humbled himself, and became obedient unto death, even the death of the cross. (Philippians 2:8)

The reason He became a human was to give His body, His life, as a propitiatory sacrifice to God for man's sin. Since God is Spirit, He cannot die. Though He lowered Himself to take on a human body so He could literally experience death, after His resurrection, Christ was exalted in a resurrected glorious body.

17

THE HOLY SPIRIT IS A PERSON

———◆———

The qualifications for someone to be called a person are that he is conscious (self-aware) of himself and others, having a mind, a will, and emotions.

The Father and the Son are consistently presented in Scripture as two subjects with their own identities. The Comforter (also called the Helper), the Holy Spirit, is presented in the same way. John 4:24 says, "God is a Spirit."

Although Spirit is neutral in the Greek language, John links the Spirit with the masculine pronoun "he" (John 14:16; 15:26; 16:8,13), giving Him a separate identity from the Son and the Father. He is also identified as "I" in Acts 13:2. The Holy Spirit is portrayed as a personal being with a self-identity different from both the Father and the Son. In the Acts passage, He (the Spirit) says:

> As they ministered to the Lord, and fasted, the Holy Ghost said, Separate *me* Barnabas and

Saul for the work whereunto *I* have called them. (emphasis added)

The main purpose of the Holy Spirit is to come alongside the believer to do what Jesus did when He was here physically, but mainly to do these things from the inside of us. Romans 8:9 says that the Holy Spirit dwells in us. This would be a hard thing to do if the Holy Spirit is just an impersonal force. He is called the Comforter and a teacher (John 14:16-17). He is a convictor of sin (John 16: 7-11). If He were impersonal, He could not duplicate all the things of Jesus, who is truly both human and God? Looking at the attributes of the Spirit, we find no difference in His nature, function, and communion with the believer from that of Jesus. He points to Jesus, not to Himself, in the same way that Jesus points to the Father. It is the Spirit who brings a person to recognize who Christ is. The Spirit has a different position, functioning in a submissive role to Christ, just as Christ was in a submissive position to the Father while on Earth. In the Scriptures, we do not find the Holy Spirit acting independently when He is sent to Earth but rather taking a subordinate position to both the Father and Christ the Son (John 16:13).

The Holy Spirit also hears from the Father (John 16:13), and He testifies of the Son, which means He is a different person from both the Father and the Son (John 15:26). We find that the Holy Spirit, as said in Romans 8:14-15, leads us to cry out Abba Father. Romans 8:26-27 says He groans with us, and He intercedes for us to the Father, putting into words what we cannot express. All these actions demonstrate that He is a person with personality, feelings, and the ability to speak.

> And because ye are sons, God hath sent forth the Spirit of his Son into your hearts, crying, Abba, Father. (Galatians 4:6)

Through prayer, the Holy Spirit is another advocate in our relationship with God the Father.

Scripture equates the Holy Spirit to God, and the following Scriptures affirm that He is *in* every born-again believer:

> But ye are not in the flesh, but in the Spirit, if so be that the Spirit of God dwell in you. Now if any man have not the Spirit of Christ, he is none of his. (Romans 8:9)

> Know ye not that ye are the temple of God, and that the Spirit of God dwelleth in you? (1 Corinthians 3:16)

> What? know ye not that your body is the temple of the Holy Ghost which is in you, which ye have of God, and ye are not your own? (1 Corinthians 6:19)

Hebrews 9:14 calls Him the eternal Spirit. 1 Corinthians 2:10 says the Spirit searches the deep things of God. He leads us, as Galatians 5:18 and Romans 8:9-14 indicate. He is our guide (John 16:13). He has a *mind*, proving He is personal

(Romans 8:27). He has the emotion of love (Romans 15:30). He can be insulted (Hebrews 10:29). He can be lied to (Acts 5:3). He can be grieved (Ephesians 4:30), and He can be blasphemed against (Matthew 12:31-32).

Evangelist and teacher Rev. R. A. Torrey (1856-1926) sums it up well:

> The Holy Spirit is a Person! The Scriptures make this plain beyond a question to any one who candidly goes to the Scriptures to find out what they really teach. Theoretically, most of us believe this, but do we in our real thought of Him, in our practical attitude toward Him, treat Him as a Person? Do we regard Him as indeed as real a Person as Jesus Christ, as loving, as wise, as strong, as worthy of our confidence and love and surrender as He?

> Do we realize that He walks by our side every day and hour? Yes, and better than that, that He dwells in our hearts and is ready to fill them? Do we know the "communion of the Holy Ghost?" (2 Corinthians 13:14). Communion means fellowship, partnership, comradeship. Do we know this personal fellowship, this partnership, this comradeship, this intimate friendship of the Holy Spirit? Herein lies the secret of a real Christian life, a life of liberty and joy and power and fullness. To have as one's ever-present Friend, and to be conscious that one has as his ever-present Friend, the Holy Spirit, and to surrender one's life

in all its departments entirely to His control, this is true Christian living.[13]

Indeed, the Holy Spirit is a person, and He is essential to Christian living. Without Him, we would have no power to live the Christian life with victory over sin. To be born again means to be born of the Spirit, with Him dwelling (abiding) in us. He enlightens our eyes that we may understand the things of God, gives us power for holy living, guides us, comforts us, and grants us assurance of salvation.

Yet I am the LORD thy God from the land of Egypt, and thou shalt know no god but me: for there is no saviour beside me. (Hosea 13:4)

18

WHO IS THE SAVIOR?

The Old Testament is absolutely clear when it states that God alone is Savior, as it is written:

> For I am the LORD thy God, the Holy One of Israel, thy Saviour. (Isaiah 43:3)

> I, even I, am the LORD; and beside me there is no saviour. (Isaiah 43:11)

> [T]here is no God else beside me; a just God and a Saviour; there is none beside me. (Isaiah 45:21)

> Look unto me, and be ye saved, all the ends of the earth: for I am God, and there is none else. (Isaiah 45:22)

> [A]nd he shall send them a saviour. (Isaiah 19:20)

God, as the only Savior, is an established doctrine in the Old Testament. When we come to New Testament revelation, we find the same God as the Savior, this time come in the flesh—Jesus. According to 1 John 4:14, this is the Son. The apostle John, one of the original twelve apostles who walked with Jesus, touched Him, and listened to His teachings from His own lips, writes:

> And we have seen and do testify that the Father sent the Son to be the Saviour of the world.

So, the Son of God, Jesus, was sent to be the Savior of the world. Yet, we are told that God alone is the Savior. Logic and biblical sense show us that the Son has to be God if He is also the Savior.

In Titus 2:13, Jesus is called our "great God and our Saviour." Titus 3:4-6 starts with, "But after that the kindness and love of *God our Saviour* toward man appeared" (emphasis added) and concludes with "Jesus Christ our Saviour" (also in Titus 1:4 and 2 Timothy 1:10). All of these New Testament references agree with those of the Old Testament.

If one does not believe that Jesus is God, then he cannot agree with Jude who writes:

> [T]o the only wise God our Saviour, be glory and majesty, dominion and power, both now and ever. Amen. (Jude 1:25)

As the apostle Peter writes:

> . . . to them that have obtained like precious faith
> with us through the righteousness of God and our
> Saviour Jesus Christ. (2 Peter 1:1)

Notice that they obtained precious faith by believing that Jesus is our God and our Savior. Salvation is found in an eternal person, who is God the Son. Christ cannot be Savior unless He is Lord (Yahweh), the Son of God. To be confused on the nature of God affects our relationship toward Him. It was God the Son who died for our sins by becoming a man, and it was God the Father who accepted that one sacrifice. By resurrecting Him, placing him at His right hand where He intercedes for His church, He continues in His eternal priesthood because His priesthood is unchangeable based on an endless life (Hebrews 7:16, 24). The book of Hebrews identifies the Son as "the author of eternal salvation unto all them that obey him" (Hebrews 5:9-11).

> And this is life eternal, that they might know thee
> the only true God, and Jesus Christ, whom thou
> hast sent. (John 17:3)

The same apostle John later writes in his epistle:

> And we know that the Son of God is come, and
> hath given us an understanding, that we may know
> him that is true, and we are in him that is true,
> even in his Son Jesus Christ. This is the true God,
> and eternal life. (1 John 5:20)

To know Jesus, whom the Father has sent, is to know the true God.

It is the Son who died for all mankind; the Father and the Spirit did not. The Son came in human flesh, while the other two never came in the flesh. Each person of the triune Godhead has a different position and function, yet none act on their own. They are in complete unity. In the Bible, there are never more than three mentioned as God. All three are involved in creation and the redemption of man.

> [F]or we shall all stand before the judgment seat of Christ. For it is written, As I live, saith the Lord, every knee shall bow to me, and every tongue shall confess to God. (Romans 14:10-11)

Part of that verse is from Isaiah 45:23 and is also quoted by Paul in Philippians 2:9-11 and applied to Jesus. To believe in the Gospel means we recognize Jesus' deity and bow our knee to Him now.

> The grace of the Lord Jesus
> Christ, and the love of God,
> and the communion of the
> Holy Ghost, be with you all.
> Amen. (2 Corinthians 13:14)

AFTERWORD

A NEW AGE VIEW OF THE TRINITY ENTERS THE CHURCH

———————◆———————

While this book has been my effort in showing how the Bible, throughout, portrays and defends the Trinitarian view (a triune nature of God), one other aspect needs to be examined. Today, the word Trinity, or Trinitarian theology, is taking on a whole new meaning, one of which most Christians are unaware but one that is working its way into the church through the highly popular book, *The Shack*. Let me explain. Many people have defended their admiration for *The Shack*, saying it is "just a novel." But *Shack* author William Paul Young admits that *The Shack* is more than a novel; he considers it a theological book:

> Please don't misunderstand me; *The Shack* is theology. But it is theology wrapped in story.[1]

Young said these words in a book written by C. Baxter Kruger titled *The Shack Revisited* where Young wrote the foreword. He also stated in the foreword:

> If you want to understand better the perspectives
> and theology that frame *The Shack,* this book
> [Kruger's] is for you. Baxter has taken on the
> incredible task of exploring the nature and character
> of the God who met me in my own shack.[2]

Reading through *The Shack Revisited,* it becomes clear
that Baxter's main theme is what he calls "the trinitarian life."

> [Jesus] became what we are, entered into our
> world of confusion. . . . He found his way into
> our darkness, into the scary places inside our souls.
> And there he pitched his tent forever—and he
> brought his Papa [the Father] and the Holy Spirit
> with him. . . . inside of us all, because of Jesus, is
> nothing short of the very trinitarian life of God.
> . . . "I am good" because Jesus and his Father and
> the Holy Spirit have found me and live in me.[3]

Contrary to what I have described about the Trinity in
this book, Baxter's (and Young's) view of the Trinity is not
just about the shared deity of the Father, Son, and Holy Spirit. Rather it encompasses all of humanity and all of creation:

> From all eternity, God is not alone and solitary,
> but lives as Father, Son, and Spirit in a rich and
> glorious fellowship of utter oneness. . . . The
> trinitarian life is a great dance of unchained
> communion and intimacy . . . This life is unique,
> and it is good and right. . . . And this love,
> giving rise to such togetherness and fellowship

and oneness, is the womb of the universe and of
humanity within it.[4]

In presenting this view of the Trinity that there is
"oneness" and "togetherness" throughout the universe and
all humanity, Kruger introduces the idea that there is no
separation between God and His creation:

> The New Testament's witness to Jesus leads to a
> revolution in human understanding of God as the
> blessed Trinity. It also leads to a revolution in our
> understanding of creation and of human existence
> as not separated from the triune God, but together
> with God in relationship forever. . . .

> The triune God, the human race, and all creation
> are not separated but together in relationship. Jesus
> is the relationship. In his own being, the Father,
> the Holy Spirit, and all creation are together.[5]

This is classic New Age panentheistic thought that teaches that God is in all things and all people, that everything is
sacred (filled with divinity), and that there is no gap between
God and man and God and creation. While we would
expect this kind of belief in the New Age, it is absolutely
contradictory to biblical Christianity. Yet, the author of one
of the most popular Christian books today has come right
out and stated that Kruger's book is the framework of *The
Shack*. Kruger further explains this trinitarian "theology":

> This means that the mutual indwelling of the
> blessed Trinity now includes us! In Jesus, the

human race has been gathered into the Holy Spirit's world. . . . the staggering oneness of the blessed Trinity, have found us in our shacks—us: you, me, all of us—forever.[6]

The very identity of Jesus Christ as the One in whom the Father, the Holy Spirit, and *all creation are bound together* carries profound geopolitical, racial, social, environmental, economic, and educational implications . . . As the Creator incarnate, Jesus, in his relationship with his Father in the Spirit, is integral to *every sphere and area* of human life and of the life of our planet. Nothing was left behind when he ascended.[7] (emphasis added)

Kruger states that "heaven and earth are united"[8] and that "the life and oneness of the blessed Trinity have crossed the infinite divide and embraced us forever."[9] This is reminiscent of the New Age idiom "as above, so below" meaning that there is no gap between God in Heaven and His creation on earth. If this were true, then Jesus' sacrifice on the Cross would have been unnecessary. Kruger continues:

Jesus has included us in his relationship with his Father, and in his relationship with the Holy Spirit, and in his relationship *with every person*, and in his relationship with *all creation*. Jesus is the center of it all. . . .

We are not separated from the blessed Trinity, but included in the trinitarian life. This is our identity, the truth of our being, and our destiny of joy.[10]

William Paul Young not only admitted in the foreword of Kruger's book that *The Shack* is based on Kruger's panentheistic ideas on the Trinity, Young also presented the idea of what he calls "the lie of separation" on a television series on TBN in 2017 when he stated:

> [I]t is a "lie" to believe that God is "separate" from His creation.[11]

Former New Age follower, Warren B. Smith, explains this "lie of separation":

> In the New Age, we didn't believe in a real Satan. The only thing "satanic" was to *not* believe in the divine "Oneness" of all creation. The only "Satan" were those who were under "the illusion of separation"—those who did not believe that God was "in" everyone and everything.[12]

Read a few quotes by one who is accepted as the New Age "Christ" who reveals himself in various channeled writings:

> The recognition of God is the recognition of yourself. There is no separation of God and His creation.[13]—*A Course in Miracles*

> The oneness of the Creator and the creation is your wholeness, your sanity and your limitless power.[14]—*A Course in Miracles*

Let Me take you with Me, My friends, back to your Source, back to the cradle of your Being, and release in you your Godhead.[15]—Maitreya

I shall drive from this Earth forever the curse of hatred, the sin of separation.[16]—Maitreya

The only solution is the Ultimate Truth: nothing exists in the universe that is separate from anything else—The "God" who spoke to Neale Donald Walsch, author of *Conversations with God.*[17]

This is your assignment. This is your work. You are to destroy the illusion of separation.[18]—Neale Donald Walsch's "God"

As we are witnessing a growing apostasy in the church, which the Bible says will happen in the days before Christ's return, a New Age spirit and false "Christ" who proclaims that God is in everything and everyone and there is no separation between God and man will continue to make himself known to the world. Paul warned about those who worship "the creature more than the Creator" (see Romans 1:23-25) in not recognizing that God and creation are truly separate and always will be. Unfortunately, many who proclaim to be Christians will fall for this lie. God, indeed, is separate from His creation. He is Father, Son, and Holy Spirit. He is not humanity, and He is not creation.

DID JESUS IDENTIFY HIMSELF AS GOD?

◆

No prophet, other than Jesus, could have said with authority, "he that believeth on me shall never thirst" or "he that believeth on me hath everlasting life" (John 6:35 & 47). No one but Jesus could have said with that same authority, "follow me" (Luke 18:22). Nor could any other prophet state, with signs and wonders proving his authority, that there are eternal consequences for not believing He is just who He claimed to be. When Jesus said, "[F]or if ye believe not that I am *he*,* ye shall die in your sins" (John 8:24), it was the definitive statement of His very being. In fact, this declaration of His is the crux of the entire Christian faith.

It is recorded in the Gospels 23 times that Jesus said, "I am," seven of which are specifically stated to identify His deity.

---

*The word "he" does not appear in the original (Greek) text but was added later in italics for readability.

In fact, if one were to truly seek to understand the deity of Christ in the Gospels, John's is the perfect place to start. It is here we begin to fully understand what Jesus meant when He applied to Himself the name "I AM," the name that God revealed to Moses at the miracle of the burning bush, recorded in the Book of Exodus.

THE DISTINCTIVE NATURE OF
THE "I AM" STATEMENTS

In the Book of Exodus, where God first appeared to Moses when he turned aside from tending his flock to see the miracle of the burning bush, Moses asked the LORD:

> Behold, when I come unto the children of Israel, and shall say unto them, The God of your fathers hath sent me unto you; and they shall say to me, What is his name? what shall I say unto them?

> And God said unto Moses, I AM THAT I AM: and he said, Thus shalt thou say unto the children of Israel, I AM hath sent me unto you. (Exodus 3:13-14)

God's own name for Himself—I AM—means the self-existent One. This I AM in the Hebrew is YHWH, where we get the name Yahweh. The Hebrew of Exodus 3:14 is *hayah asher hayah*, meaning, I AM THAT I AM. The name is stated as *ego eimi* in the LXX Septuagint (the Greek translation of the Hebrew Old Testament).

In the New Testament, Jesus applied to Himself the name I AM to demonstrate His claim to deity. The I AM statements are made with a predicate, and the Greek words ego eimi used by John are distinct and applied only to Jesus.

It is crucial to an understanding of the New Testament to realize that the Jewish audience to whom Jesus spoke knew immediately that His "I AM" statements referred directly to the name of God revealed to Moses in the Book of Exodus. They understood fully that He was appropriating the name I AM because He claimed to be the God of the Old Testament. This, specifically, was why the Jewish leaders accused Him of blasphemy and picked up stones to stone Him to death—"that thou, being a man, makest thyself God" (John 10:33).

John 8:56-59 contains perhaps the most direct reference to Jesus' deity. In this confrontation with His Jewish listeners recorded immediately after He forgave the woman caught in adultery, Jesus said:

> Your father Abraham rejoiced to see my day: and he saw it, and was glad. Then said the Jews unto him, Thou art not yet fifty years old, and hast thou seen Abraham? Jesus said unto them, Verily, verily, I say unto you, Before Abraham was, I am. Then took they up stones to cast at him.

In this passage, it would be a massive mistake, both grammatically and theologically, to take Jesus' words as meaning merely that He existed from or before Abraham's time. This was not the meaning at all. Here, Jesus is directly saying, "Yahweh is my name."

Jesus made a definitive statement that before Abraham came into existence or was born, He (Jesus) already was. His "I AM" reference conveys the thought, "I have existed before all ages; before anything was created I existed. My existence is eternal, without respect to time. I AM THAT I AM."

But Jesus made an absolute claim to be God and confirmed it by His resurrection. Hence, only He is the Savior of the world (John 4:42).

> And Jesus answered and said unto them, Take heed
> that no man deceive you. For many shall come in
> my name, saying, I am Christ; and shall deceive
> many. (Matthew 24:4-5)

CHRIST REVEALED HIMSELF
AS OUR ETERNAL FOOD

am the bread of life" (John 6:35). This is the first of the "I AM" proclamations contained in the Book of John, said in the discourse which followed the feeding of the multitude. During the discourse, Jesus told the crowd:

> Labour not for the meat which perisheth, but for
> that meat which endureth unto everlasting life,
> which the Son of man shall give unto you: for him
> hath God the Father sealed. (John 6:27).

As He sought to elicit faith in Himself, He was met with a challenge to "demonstrate His credentials," so to speak. They asked him, "What sign showest thou then, that we may see, and believe thee?" To this they added, "Our fathers did eat manna in the desert; as it is written, He [Moses] gave them bread from heaven to eat" (vv. 30-31). With this verse, the people referred to the Book of Exodus, where God rained down manna from Heaven to feed them.

But Jesus corrected their misunderstanding when He stated:

> Verily, verily, I say unto you, Moses gave you not
> that bread from heaven; but my Father giveth you
> the true bread from heaven. For the bread of God
> is he which cometh down from heaven, and giveth
> life unto the world. (John 6:32-33)

With this, Christ reminded them to think in spiritual terms, not earthly ones as they were doing, having just recently come from the miracle of the loaves and the fishes. In fact, they were not asking for the bread from Heaven, which is how Jesus was offering Himself. They wanted an earthly king and were overjoyed to have one who could perform miracles to their earthly benefit. In response to their request of "Lord, evermore give us this bread" (v. 34), Jesus made the claim:

> I am the bread of life: he that cometh to me shall
> never hunger; and he that believeth on me shall
> never thirst. (John 6:35)

In their long sojourn with Moses, the Israelites had two constant complaints—hunger and thirst. But in the Book of John, Jesus is not speaking of the physical but the spiritual, referring to Himself as the answer to the needs of the human heart. He alone is our source of spiritual nourishment. Since bread is a basic food, His statements claim that He came to fulfill this role for everyone. He is the "Saviour of the world" (John 4:42) and gives life to the world (John 6:33). Jesus alone is the bread of life. All other bread satisfies earthly hunger, and that only temporarily. Physically, one will hunger again; like the manna in the wilderness which was good for the day it was given but not for the next day. It would sustain them for a day, but did nothing for them long-term. With Christ, however, the salvation He provides is everlasting, and once tasted, those receiving it will be eternally satisfied. As Jesus said in verse 51:

> I am the living bread which came down from heaven: if any man eat of this bread, he shall live for ever.

Jesus identified Himself as the sustenance man needs to survive in order to be preserved from eternal death and separation from God. When Jesus said to the people, "I am the bread of life," and "the bread of God is he which cometh down from heaven," He is making His heavenly origins known.

CHRIST REVEALED HIMSELF AS OUR LIGHT

In the beginning of his Gospel, John introduces us to Jesus as both the light and life, declaring in chapter one, verses 3-5:

> All things were made by him; and without him was not any thing made that was made. In him

was life; and the life was the light of men. And
the light shineth in darkness; and the darkness
comprehended it not.

Darkness in the above verse is representative of what is
fallen and what is ignorance or sin.

The apostle wrote to us that Jesus is the revelation of
truth and salvation for everyone:

He [John the Baptist] was not that Light, but was
sent to bear witness of that Light. That was the
true Light, which lighteth every man that cometh
into the world. (John 1:8-9)

In His second "I AM" statement, Jesus once again picks
up the light metaphor and expands on what had been previously written, affirming that He is the true light, the light
of all men. John 8:12 states:

Then spake Jesus again unto them, saying, I am the
light of the world: he that followeth me shall not
walk in darkness, but shall have the light of life.

John tells us Jesus made this claim at the Feast of
Tabernacles in the Temple courts. The backdrop to the
Feast of Tabernacles is important, as two major symbolic
ceremonies took place. The first was the outpouring of water
on the steps by the Levitical priests, as the choir sang the
Great Hallel (Psalms 113-118). The second was the lighting
of several large candelabra (menorahs) in the Temple area,
which lit up the Temple with a light that could be seen

for miles. Jesus took the opportunity of using these two ritualistic symbols to illustrate His teachings and person (John 7:37-38; 8:12).

In the eighth chapter of the Book of John, where Jesus spoke of Himself as the light of the world, He taught in the Court of the Women, which was the most public part of the temple. Four golden candelabra stood there with golden bowls filled with oil. These were lit on the first night of the Feast of Tabernacles (in reference to the memory of the pillar of cloud by day and of fire by night). The figure itself was familiar to all, drawn from prophecy and tradition. According to Hebrew tradition, God is light, and Light was one of the names of Messiah, as well as a reference to His work among His people (Isaiah 9:2, 42:6, Malachi 4:2; Luke 2:32; John 8:12; John 9:5; 1 John 1:5).

God is described as light or being clothed in light. Isaiah 60:19 reminds us that "the LORD shall be unto thee an everlasting light, and thy God thy glory." Psalm 104:2 states that God is the One who "coverest thyself with light as with a garment." In 1 Corinthians 2:8, the apostle Paul declares Jesus to be the "Lord of glory," a term denoting His deity because it refers to God's *shekinah*, His light.

With this as the background, Jesus' exclusive claim of being the light of the whole world was, in effect, a proclamation that He was the fulfillment of their Jewish faith, a very exclusive faith given to them by God.

The light metaphor is also found in Old Testament events and typology. The glory (the presence of God) in the cloud led the Hebrews to the Promised Land (Exodus 13:21-22) and protected them from their enemies (Exodus 14:19-25). The Israelites sang, "The LORD is my light and my salvation" (Psalm 27:1). Isaiah the Prophet tells us that the Servant of the LORD (Messiah) was given as a light to the Gentiles, that He might bring salvation to the ends of the earth (Isaiah 49:6). The coming Millennial Age will be a time when the LORD Himself will be the light of His people (Isaiah 60:19-20; Revelation 21:23-24).

Jesus' declaration at the Temple made it clear who He is. He is not the light of the Jews only, but "the light of the world." His reference to being the light of every man bespeaks that those who reject Him reject God, and that a person's eternal destiny depends on his acknowledgment and acceptance of who Jesus claims to be.

In light of all these Scriptures, it is evident that one cannot praise God in truth, and yet deny the deity of Jesus, the Son of God.

CHRIST REVEALED HIMSELF AS THE DOOR

I am the door: by me if any man enter in, he shall be saved, and shall go in and out, and find pasture" (John 10:9).

To "be saved" means "to have eternal life," which only God can give. Jesus, in His third "I AM" statement, is therefore saying, "I am the Door" or "the way in," referring to His deity.

Jesus often spoke in parables (v. 6), which consist of some prominent metaphors. For example, "sheepfold" (v. 10:1), "shepherd" (v. 2), "porter" (watchman) (v. 3), "door," or "gate" (v. 7). The door is the entry into a house or a place of safety.

A shepherd in charge of his flock has to be constantly vigilant. In biblical times, he would lay himself down in front of the only way in or out of the sheep pen, in order to guard the flock. Anything approaching the sheep's place of safety would first have to pass over him. In reference to this, Jesus begins His discourse by saying in verse 1:

> Verily, verily, I say unto you, He that entereth not
> by the door into the sheepfold, but climbeth up
> some other way, the same is a thief and a robber.

So we see that Jesus is saying that only He, and no other, is the means by which the sheep (those who accept Him as Lord and Savior) may enter into the promised fullness of life. To emphasize this, He continues in John 10:10:

> The thief cometh not, but for to steal, and to kill,
> and to destroy: I am come that they might have
> life, and that they might have it more abundantly.

CHRIST REVEALED HIMSELF AS OUR SHEPHERD

I am the good shepherd: the good shepherd giveth his life for the sheep" (John 10:11). In His fourth "I AM" statement, Jesus shows the depths of His love for us. He adds an adjective to the word shepherd, and that is the word "good." Here again Jesus is contrasting Himself with the religious leaders to whom He is speaking. Such leaders demonstrated that they were not good shepherds, but rather, they are called in this chapter "hirelings," a derogatory term. A hireling is a shepherd who works only for pay and cares nothing for the actual health of the sheep (v. 12-13), and who will, in fact, run away at the first sign of danger.

When Jesus used the term "the good shepherd," He was speaking of His intrinsic goodness, His moral nature and beauty. The word shepherd demonstrates a position of authority over the sheep—that is, the people who come to Him in faith. He rules over all, of course, believer and unbeliever alike, but in this passage, He shows His goodness toward those who are His own. As the Good Shepherd, He protects, warns, leads, guides, and nourishes the sheep in His charge. In turn, we (the sheep) admit our utter defenselessness and total dependence on Him.

King David made the allusion to this concept beautifully in his 23rd Psalm when he said in the first verse, "The LORD is my shepherd; I shall not want."

In modern terms this means that David said, "I have everything I need in You, Lord. I shall have no lack whatsoever."

In His Good Shepherd analogy, Jesus is also referring to His mission. In at least three verses (15, 17, and 18), He speaks of "laying down" His life for the sheep, meaning that He protects them to the point of death, which was accomplished literally at His crucifixion. His wonderful love encompasses all who come to Him in faith, whether Jew or Gentile.

The shepherd of the Old Testament was found to be both a leader and a companion to his sheep. First Samuel 17:34-37 is a remarkable example of the young David, who is an Old Testament prefigure of Christ protecting His sheep. The shepherd knows his flock and is gentle with them (Proverbs 27:23). The shepherd carries the lambs in his arms (Isaiah 40:11), rescues them from those who abuse them (Ezekiel 34:11-22), and seeks them out when they wander away (Isaiah 53:6).

In New Testament references, Matthew 11:28 reveals the heart of our Shepherd for those who belong to Him, promising rest for the weary. One of our Lord's most famous parables is of the shepherd who seeks after the lost sheep (Luke 15:1-7).

In John 10:16, Jesus states that He builds His flock, and they shall be one flock with Him as the Shepherd over them. This He speaks concerning His salvation, words which would mean nothing had He not shown Himself repeatedly to be the Son of God. John the Baptist referred to Christ as the only sacrifice for sins when he declared, "Behold the Lamb of God, which taketh away the sin of the world" (John 1:29). So, by His sacrifice, once for all, has salvation come to all who receive Him. Again, presenting Himself as the sinless sacrifice, Jesus shows clearly His deity.

In addition to the John 10 discourse, Jesus is called, "the Shepherd and Bishop of your souls" (1 Peter 2:25), the "Chief Shepherd" (1 Peter 5:4), and the "Great Shepherd" (Hebrews 13:20).

The mercy of the Great Shepherd is exemplified in Matthew 9:36:

> But when he saw the multitudes, he was moved with compassion on them, because they fainted, and were scattered abroad, as sheep having no shepherd.

As the Shepherd of the sheep (Christians), Jesus has declared Himself the One whom the sheep are to follow. He makes it perfectly clear that those who refuse to follow

Him refuse to follow God; and if they do not follow Jesus, then they are not His sheep. As He said in John 10:27-30:

> My sheep hear my voice, and I know them, and they follow me: and I give unto them eternal life; and they shall never perish, neither shall any man pluck them out of my hand. My Father, which gave them me, is greater than all; and no man is able to pluck them out of my Father's hand. I and my Father are one.

The response to these words by His pharisaical listeners is startling—"Then the Jews took up stones again to stone him" (John 10:31).

Unrepentant sinners and mockers can weave all the lies and confusion they want, denying that Christ ever called Himself God, but their denials are meaningless in light of the Jews' response to Jesus. The Jews of Jesus' time knew perfectly well what He meant in His "shepherd's" discourse. They knew He was identifying Himself with the character and nature of God.

> For a good work we stone thee not; but for blasphemy; and because that thou, being a man, makest thyself God (verse 33).

In the magnificent context of His salvation for those who receive Him, Jesus is not only the Shepherd but the Lamb, God's one sacrifice for sin forever. He is the same one Shepherd from the Old Testament continuing into the New Testament (e.g., Psalm 23, Zechariah 13:7).

Christ's declaration of exclusivity as the Shepherd sent by God demonstrated that He was the fulfillment of these prophecies (John 10:8, 11, 14).

> For the Lamb which is in the midst of the throne shall feed them, and shall lead them unto living fountains of waters: and God shall wipe away all tears from their eyes. (Revelation 7:17)

CHRIST REVEALED HIMSELF AS THE RESURRECTION AND THE LIFE

> I am the resurrection, and the life: he that believeth in me, though he were dead, yet shall he live: and whosoever liveth and believeth in me shall never die. Believest thou this? (John 11:25-26)

The one main hope of mankind is that physical death is not the end, that the grave is not the final statement of man's futility, but rather that life is eternal, continuing forever. In John 11:21-26, Jesus stood before a weeping Martha, whose brother Lazarus had died four days earlier. He told her that her brother, who was also Jesus' friend, would rise again. She misunderstood, thinking He meant the final resurrection at the Last Day. But with the assurance only God gives, Jesus replied:

> I am the resurrection, and the life: he that believeth in me, though he were dead, yet shall he live: and

whosoever liveth and believeth in me shall never
die. Believest thou this?

Here, in this astonishing declaration, Jesus states that
He not only imparts life, but that He is Life. His being the
Resurrection means that even if death lays claim on a believer, it will not be a permanent death, but one which will
be swallowed up by eternal life.

This is not the first time in John's Gospel that Jesus
spoke of His authority over death. After He had cleansed
the Temple, driving out the moneychangers and cattle with
a whip of cords He had made, the irate Jews demanded a
sign of His authority to do so. He declared:

> Destroy this temple, and in three days I will raise
> it up . . . But he spake of the temple of his body.
> (John 2:19, 21)

And again, in His Good Shepherd discourse, Jesus made
clear His absolute authority over death when He said:

> Therefore doth my Father love me, because I lay
> down my life, that I might take it again. No man
> taketh it from me, but I lay it down of myself. I
> have power to lay it down, and I have power to
> take it again. This commandment have I received
> of my Father. (John 10:17-18)

In this scriptural passage, Jesus declares Himself Lord
over even death, not just the death of others, but over His
own physical death which would be accomplished on the

Cross. None but God could make such statements and verify them by doing what He said He would do.

JESUS REVEALED HIMSELF AS THE
WAY, THE TRUTH, AND THE LIFE

In the fourteenth chapter of John, Jesus reveals Himself more fully to those closest to Him—the remaining eleven disciples with whom He just celebrated the Passover feast, prior to His suffering and death. Foretelling His leaving them by way of the crucifixion, Jesus reminds them that "whither I go ye know, and the way ye know" (v. 4).

Thomas, unfairly known as "the doubter," desires further explanation, and Jesus replies, "I am the way, the truth, and the life: no man cometh unto the Father, but by me" (John 14:6).

In this further, three-part declaration of His nature and earthly mission, Jesus reiterates that only through Him can men be saved, thus again declaring Himself to be God.

Jesus' reference in John 14:2 to His Father's house indicates a very specific place—one only for believers in Him. The way of salvation is the only way that leads to the Father, and receiving His Son for the forgiveness of sins is the only way to be taken to His Father's place of dwelling (His "house"). This entire biblical passage speaks again of Christ's exclusivity, a term much derided in our politically-correct society but one which is nonetheless accurate. Contrary to popular *un*belief, the so-called "many paths to God" do not exist. Jesus said, "[N]arrow is the way, which leadeth unto life, and few there be that find it" (Matthew 7:14). Buddha, Mohammed, Confucius, Lao Tzu, and innumerable other religious prophets lead their devoted, but lost, followers *away* from "the Way," the salvation which Jesus assured us comes through Him only. It is only through humbly receiving Him and believing in His death and resurrection that sinners can be reconciled to God. This is what is called the Gospel. When Jesus said, "I AM the way, the truth, and the life," He also explained, "No man cometh unto the Father, but by me" (John 14:6). Jesus is not one of many ways to God that we can choose from, but the *only* way for all time.

Speaking of Himself as "the Truth" means that His words, hence His character and His deity, are unalterable. Whatever the Father gave Jesus to do and to say, He did perfectly, and His revealing of the Father to us can be trusted without reservation. Not only because He tells the truth but because He is truth incarnate (John 1:1, 14), His word is settled in Heaven forever (Psalm 119:89). The complete revelation of God is declared in Him (John 1:18), and the Bible properly calls Him God.

Jesus' declaration of Himself as "the Life" reaffirms what He said about Himself in previous chapters, indicating that He is able to give life to those who are both spiritually and physically dead. He said it would be His voice the dead would hear and respond to on the Last Day (John 5:28-29). Showing Himself to be God, He stated:

> For as the Father raiseth up the dead, and quickeneth [gives life to] them; even so the Son quickeneth [gives life to] whom he will. (John 5:21)

This, then, is yet another statement of exclusivity, a position reserved for Jesus alone. He alone is the way to God; and through His historically documented resurrection, He has proven Himself completely reliable. He stands in a relation to truth that no one else does.

Again, when Jesus used the "I AM" construction by itself or attached to an Old Testament example, He was indicating His divinity. John communicates this in various manners to show who the Messiah is from the Old Testament background.

JESUS REVEALED HIMSELF AS THE TRUE VINE

Many Old Testament analogies relate to the vine and the vineyard. The vine was often used as a symbol of the nation of Israel, and God is depicted as the vinedresser who both planted the vine and tends it. This can be seen in the following passages of Scripture:

> Thou hast brought a vine out of Egypt: thou hast cast out the heathen, and planted it. Thou preparedst room before it, and didst cause it to take deep root, and it filled the land (Psalm 80:8-9).

> For the vineyard of the LORD of hosts is the house of Israel, and the men of Judah his pleasant plant. (Isaiah 5:7)

In His teaching to His disciples just prior to being arrested, Jesus spoke also of the vine and vinedresser, an Old

Testament analogy of which they would have been well aware. He told them:

> I am the true vine, and my Father is the husbandman [vinedresser]. Every branch in me that beareth not fruit he taketh away: and every branch that beareth fruit, he purgeth [cleanses, prunes] it, that it may bring forth more fruit. (John 15:1-2)

There is an intimacy here—the final, loving, encouraging words to His remaining disciples (Judas had already left to betray Him). He tells them to cleave to Him, to hold onto Him in unshakable faith, to "abide" in Him as He said in verses 4-5:

> Abide in me, and I in you. As the branch cannot bear fruit of itself, except it abide in the vine; no more can ye, except ye abide in me. I am the vine, ye are the branches: He that abideth in me, and I in him, the same bringeth forth much fruit: for without me ye can do nothing.

There again is His exclusive declaration of His deity. Without Him, we can do nothing of spiritual significance.

In the Old Testament, the "vine" was Israel. All who wanted a saving relationship with God had to be "grafted," so to speak, into Israel—physically by circumcision and spiritually by adhering to the Law. But as Israel repeatedly rebelled against the commands of the LORD, it was judged, often with consequences disastrous to the nation, but always with the intent to bring straying hearts back into right relationship with God (Psalm 80:15-16).

But with the appearing of Jesus, He declared Himself to be, now, the "vine," and commands that all who would henceforth come to God, must come through Christ and abide in Him as closely as branches abide in the vine to which they are attached. He being the true vine means He is our lifegiver and the One who enables us to bear "fruit" as we abide in Him. This fruit, which glorifies God (Matthew 3:8, 7:20; Romans 6:22; Galatians 5:22-23), shows that we belong to Jesus, and assists us in the faithful proclamation of the Gospel.

The transformation of the believer into Christ-like character takes place by the work of the indwelling Spirit of Christ (Romans 8:9). This "I AM" saying in John chapter 15, like the others, indicates Jesus' deity, for only God can indwell all people who receive Him.

CONCLUSION

In this unbelieving, mocking age, it seems almost everybody likes Jesus, so long as He can be made in their image. Two main stumbling blocks to most people's acceptance of the truth of the Gospel accounts are:

1) Jesus' deity—that He is, in fact, God.

2) The exclusivity—that He alone is the way of salvation.

We live in an ungodly time that glorifies relative "truth" and shuns claims of exclusivity, even if these claims are uttered by God Himself. Political correctness demands that everyone gain admittance to literally any group he or she desires, whether on Earth or in Heaven. It insists that each person is good enough on his or her own merits to earn salvation. If grace is even considered at all, it is a human construct whereby everyone is granted forgiveness of sins. "After all, we're only human." "What kind of God would punish forever those who have no interest in accepting Christ as the only way to salvation?" "Rather narrow-minded, isn't it?"

The hard fact is that the Christian path is narrow and difficult (Matthew 7:14), and comparatively few find and live by it. The Christian way is one of taking up a daily cross, as Jesus took up His (Luke 9:23), and following Christ no matter what the earthly cost. In our pleasure-oriented society, most simply are not interested in pursuing the truth of the One who maps out that difficult kind of lifestyle for His followers.

For believers in Jesus, the truths He presents, while infinitely deep, are simple to grasp by childlike faith (Matthew 18:3). Unbelievers must convince themselves otherwise only through their own exhausting efforts, which rest wholly on their ability to perform immense theological contortions. They wrest Scriptures from context, apply contrived methods of exegesis, and fit their own image of Christ into a convenient spiritual compartment, one that allows them a false comfort, and one, unfortunately, big enough to include all manner of false prophets. But for all their efforts, they are left standing before the looming, unalterable Word of God, which continues to state for all time that—

> In the beginning was the Word, and the Word was with God, and the Word was God. (John 1:1)

No man hath seen God at any time; the only begotten Son, which is in the bosom of the Father, he hath declared him. (John 1:18)

For had ye believed Moses, ye would have believed me: for he wrote of me. But if ye believe not his writings, how shall ye believe my words? (John 5:46-47, also referencing Deuteronomy 18:15-19)

[H]e that believeth on me, believeth not on me, but on him that sent me. And he that seeth me seeth him that sent me. (John 12:44-45)

[Y]e believe in God, believe also in me. (John 14:1)

[H]e that hath seen me hath seen the Father. (John 14:9)

For there is one God, and one mediator between God and men, the man Christ Jesus; who gave himself a ransom for all, to be testified in due time. (1 Timothy 2:5-6)

. . . who being the brightness of his glory, and the express image of his person, and upholding all things by the word of his power, when he had by himself purged our sins, sat down on the right hand of the Majesty on high. (Hebrews 1:3)

It is the way of this present age to encourage every people group to choose whatever gods, idols, or "masters" to which they would like to give allegiance. The world has always loved its false prophets, who speak comfort to the rebellious who indulge sin. And it shuns, often with derisive laughter, the cost of faithfulness to our Lord. Yet, through unbelievers' stubbornness, they incur to themselves a cost beyond their imagining. To the unbeliever in heart, Jesus leaves a terrifying promise:

> I go my way, and ye shall seek me, and shall die in your sins: whither I go, ye cannot come. (John 8:21)

Jesus then gave His reason for rejecting them:

> Ye are from beneath; I am from above: ye are of this world; I am not of this world. I said therefore unto you, that ye shall die in your sins: for if ye believe not that *I am he*, ye shall die in your sins. (John 8:23-24, emphasis added to "I am")

In the italicized portion above, the word "he" does not appear in the original (Greek) text but was added later for readability. Again, Jesus was identifying Himself as the I AM that Moses encountered at the burning bush. But to believers in Christ—those who come to Him in faith and hold fast His testimony—He leaves to us, as He did to the grieving Martha, this everlasting promise from John 11:25-26:

> I am the resurrection, and the life: he that believeth in me, though he were dead, yet shall he live: and whosoever liveth and believeth in me shall never die.

ENDNOTES

1. Augustus H. Strong, *Systematic Theology* (1903, Kindle edition), p.144, Kindle location 9717.

2. Harry A. Ironside, *The Holy Trinity* (Kindle edition, no date given), pp. 7-8.

3. Dave Hunt, *The Trinity* (The Berean Call, October 1, 1989, https://www.thebereancall.org/content/trinity).

4. A. T. Robertson, *Word Pictures in the New Testament* (Ephesians Four Group, 2014, Kindle edition), Kindle location 74590.

5. W. E. Vine, *The Epistles of John* (Grand Rapids, MI, Second printing, 1971), p.11.

6. Louis Berkhof, *Systematic Theology* (Louisville, KY, GLH Publishing, original copyright 1938, Kindle edition), p. 66.

7. A. T. Robertson, *Word Pictures in the New Testament*, op. cit., Kindle locations 48916, 48953, 50256, 50334.

8. Charles Hodge, *Systematic Theology* (Louisville, KY, GLH Publishing, Kindle edition of all three volumes), Kindle locations 8861, 8883.

9. J. B. Lightfoot, *The Epistle St. Paul to the Galatians* (Hendrickson Publishers, 1982 edition), p.168.

10. *International Standard Bible Encyclopedia*, p.2338-39.

11. From Jamieson, Fausset, and Brown Commentary.

12. Gregory Nazianzen (329-389 A.D.) He was known as the "Trinitarian Theologian."

13. Rev. R. A. Torrey, *The Personality and Deity of the Holy Spirit.*

AFTERWORD ENDNOTES

1. William Paul Young in the foreword to C. Baxter Kruger's book, *The Shack Revisited* (New York, NY: Faith Words, Hachette Book Group, 2012), p. xi.

2. Ibid., p. ix.

3. Ibid., p. 49.

4. Ibid., p. 62.

5. ibid., pp. 140-141.

6. Ibid., p. 141.

7. Ibid., p. 218.

8. Ibid., p. 219.

9. Ibid.

10. Ibid., p. 22.

11. *Restoring the Shack* television series, Trinity Broadcasting Network (TBN), 20 episodes that were originally broadcast from to July 9, 2017. *Restoring the Shack* online at: https://www.tbn.org/programs/restoring-shack).

12. Warren Smith, "Wm. Paul Young Teaches New Age Lie About Separation on TBN" (Lighthouse Trails Research blog, September 23, 2017, http://www.lighthousetrailsresearch.com/blog/?p=23824).

13. *A Course in Miracles,* Combined Volume [Text, Workbook for Students, Manual for Teachers] (Glen Ellen, CA: Foundation for Inner Peace, 1992), p. 147 (Text).

14. Ibid.

15. Message No. 51, November 23, 1978.

16. Ibid., p. 104.

17. Neale Donald Walsch, *Conversations with God: Book 2* (Charlottesville, VA: Hampton Roads Publishing Company, Inc., 1997), p. 173.

18. Neale Donald Walsch, *Friendship with God: An Uncommon Dialogue* (New York, NY: G. P. Putnam's Sons, 1999), p. 21.

SCRIPTURE-VERSE INDEX

TEACHING LECTURE DVDS
BY MIKE OPPENHEIMER

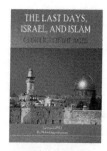

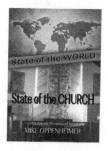

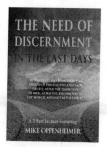

For length and pricing of these lecture DVDs, please visit our website at www.lighthousetrails.com or call, e-mail, or write and request a catalog.

THE

GOOD SHEPHERD

CALLS

BY ROGER OAKLAND

SINCE THE TURN of the millennium, in particular since September 11, 2001 when America was attacked by terrorists triggering a global-wide spiritual paradigm shift, Christianity as we have known it has experienced a major meltdown. While many are saying Christianity is on the brink of a great revival and even a "new reformation," in reality, we are witnessing the greatest apostasy in modern-day history.

The Good Shepherd Calls brings clarity to what this delusion looks like, why it is happening, where it is headed, and what can still be done to warn believers and unbelievers alike.

Released 2017 by Lighthouse Trails | $14.95 | 288 pages

OTHER BOOKS BY LIGHTHOUSE TRAILS

Another Jesus (2nd ed.)
by Roger Oakland, $12.95

A Time of Departing (2nd ed.)
by Ray Yungen, $14.95

Castles in the Sand (a novel)
by Carolyn A. Greene, $12.95

Changed by Beholding
by Harry Ironside, $11.95

Faith Undone
by Roger Oakland, $14.95

For Many Shall Come in My Name
(2nd ed.) by Ray Yungen, $13.95

Foxe's Book of Martyrs
by John Foxe
$14.95, illustrated

*How to Prepare for Hard Times &
Persecution*
by Maria Kneas, $14.95

*How to Protect Your Child from
the New Age & Spiritual Deception*
by Berit Kjos, $14.95

Let There Be Light
by Roger Oakland, $13.95

Muddy Waters
by Nanci Des Gerlaise, $14.95

Out of India
by Caryl Matrisciana, $13.95

*Simple Answers: Understanding the
Catholic Faith* by Ray Yungen, $12.95

Strength for Tough Times (2nd ed.)
by Maria Kneas, $11.95

*Taizé—A Community and Worship: Ecumenical Reconciliation or
an Interfaith Delusion?* by Chris
Lawson, $10.95

The Color of Pain
by Gregory Reid, $10.95

The Evolution Conspiracy by Roger
Oakland/Caryl Matrisciana, $14.95

The Good Shepherd Calls
by Roger Oakland, $14.95

The Gospel in Bonds
by Georgi Vins, $13.95

Things We Couldn't Say
by Diet Eman, $14.95, photos

The Other Side of the River
by Kevin Reeves, $14.95

Trapped in Hitler's Hell
by Anita Dittman
$13.95, illustrated, photos

For a complete listing of all our
books and DVDs, go to
www.lighthousetrails.com,
or request a copy of our catalog.

To order additional copies of:
The Trinity
Send $11.95 per book plus shipping:
$3.00 for 1 book, $6.00 flat rate for all other U.S. orders to:

Lighthouse Trails Publishing
P.O. Box 908
Eureka, Montana 59917

For bulk rates of 10 or more copies, contact Lighthouse Trails
Publishing, either by phone, online, e-mail, or fax. You may
order online at www.lighthousetrails.com or for US & Canada
orders, call our toll-free number: 866/876-3910.

For international and all other calls: 406/889-3610
Fax: 406/889-3633

The Trinity, as well as other books by Lighthouse Trails Publishing,
can be ordered through all major outlet stores, bookstores, online
bookstores, and Christian bookstores. Bookstores may order through:
Ingram, SpringArbor, Anchor, or directly through Lighthouse Trails.

Libraries may order through Baker & Taylor.
Quantity discounts available for most of our books.

For other resources, visit our website at:
www.lighthousetrails.com.

Also check out our extensive research site at:
www.lighthousetrailsresearch.com.

You may visit Mike Oppenheimer's website, Let Us Reason
Ministries, to access his exhaustive collection of lectures,
articles, books, CDs, and DVDs:
www.letusreason.org.

NOTES

NOTES

82894874R00078

Made in the USA
Columbia, SC
21 December 2017